I'm Tired Enough to Retire

Rose Scholl and the Children
of the
Church of the Brethren's
Mexico, Indiana
Welfare Home, 1935

Eric Flora

I'm Tired Enough to Retire

Eric Flora

ISBN (Print Edition): 978-1-54399-066-9

ISBN (eBook Edition): 978-1-54399-067-6

TABLE OF CONTENTS

ACKNOWLEDGMENTS

At the risk of leaving someone out, I am grateful to those who helped on this project. Thanks to the following for their help: Ashley Armstrong, Carol Bowman, Sharon Brooks, Christina Carey, Carroll County Historical Society, Marjorie Denton, James DeWitt, Jim DeWitt, Paula Disbro, Curtis Elburn, Jack Elburn, Joleen Flora, Mark and Evelyn Flora, Mary Beth Gast, Shirley Griffin, Lisa Haughton, Glenna Hepworth, Morris Herkless, Christy Huiras, Debra Johns, Merl and Janice Knaus, Patricia Korba, Donna Kordes, Mike Kordes, Bessie Kozma, Sandy Kraning, Sharon Linn, James McConahay, Miami County Historical Society, Charles Morgan, Barbara Olinger, Dawn Olinger, Kathy Patrick, John Potocki, Judy Runk, Gary Scholl, Marge Scholl, Arlene Siddall, Viva Jo Siddall, Mark Alan Smith, John E. & Lucille Terria, Timbercrest Senior Living Center and Selina Uglow.

Mexico Welfare Home
(James DeWitt Family)

INTRODUCTION

The names jumped out from Rose Scholl's address books. Iris Flitcraft Dale of Lebanon. Lawrence Deardorff of Monticello and Kokomo. James C. DeWitt of Culver. Pauline Foote McClain of Huntington. Thelma Gorney of Peru. Thelma Glassburn Huddleston of Logansport. Lois Miller Loop of Kokomo and Marion. Geneva DeWitt Messer of Butte, Montana. Elvera Rarick Byrket of Elkhart. Ralph Rarick of Elkhart. Alberta Wilson Schwenk of New Straitsville, Ohio and Pine River, Minnesota. Bertha Voight of Peru. And Clevo Williams Ruemler of Monticello.

Rose never talked much regarding her time at the Welfare Home. When her son-in-law, my grandfather, moved to an assisted living home I ended up with Rose's journals. Before her death, she went through her journals and scratched out sections and destroyed other journals in their entirety. Only a single diary, 1935, documenting her time at the Welfare Home survived.

Rosa "Rose" Blocher was born in July 1900 near Camden, Indiana, while William McKinley served as the twenty-fifth President. She spent most of her childhood and teenage years homesteading with her family in Ward County, North Dakota. As a young girl, her parents forbade her to marry her first love, as they didn't think he was industrious enough. He was also seventeen years older. So, two days before

Christmas 1923, she married Forrest Scholl in Ward County. Soon after they moved to a farm in Carroll County, Indiana.

They had a daughter, Anna Lou, born in January 1925, nineteen days before a six-hundred-twenty-one-mile emergency dog sled trip delivered emergency diphtheria serum at Nome, Alaska. Forrest and Rose also had a son, Robert Eugene, born in April 1927, the same year John Daniel Rust invented the mechanical cotton picker. Rose initiated divorce proceedings in June 1930. She withdrew the lawsuit in mid-October 1930. Four days later she charged Forrest with "cruel and inhuman treatment."

Forrest and Rose Scholl
1924
(Rose Scholl Family)

They finalized their divorce in September 1931, and he returned to North Dakota. Forrest allowed Rose to keep the farm and assume the one thousand five hundred dollar loan payment, which they had borrowed from John Leedy, a local minister. Rose took possession of the seventy-acre farm on the first of March 1932.

The Great Depression lasted from 1929 to 1939. By 1933 fifteen million Americans were unemployed. Some time in 1932 Rose sent her children to live with her parents, near Camden, Indiana, while she worked and lived at the Mexico Welfare Home for a dollar a day for the next four and a half years. She resigned her position at the home in September 1936. Rose died in 1995, just a few days shy of her ninety-fifth birthday. She was the great grandma who always gave us handmade cards for our birthdays and holidays. She never remarried because the Old German Baptist Church, then and now, forbade its members to divorce and remarry, based on their understanding of the scriptures.

Levi Miller donated land and a building "located on the beautiful banks of Eel river in the town of Mexico, Indiana, on the Vandalia railroad" in 1889 for an Old Folks and Orphan's Home at Mexico. "When the home was first opened the old folks and children were kept together, but it was soon discovered that the playfulness of the young ones was sometimes annoying to the elder inmates, or that the sedateness of the old served to check the natural tendency of the children to amuse themselves."

The purpose of the home was "to better provide for and take care of poor and infirm members of said church (Church of the Brethren) and orphan children of any faith, who may be duly admitted to the benefits of said Home, to train up and properly educate said orphan children and to prepare them for the proper and correct discharge of the duties of life."

In 1900, the editor of the Macy Monitor wrote he "was favorably impressed with the excellent management everywhere manifest. He has children there from almost everywhere and is fortunate in finding them homes. The work that is being done there stands at the head of philanthropic enterprises and is justified from a business standpoint by the fact that it is self-supporting."

The former Superintendent of the home, Henry Swayer, described his time at the home as "Hard heartbreaking work, continuous expansion to meet the needs of those it served." He said "Let your imagination wonder about the responsibility of caring for this many children. I have witnessed the pain and sorrow, even tears on the faces of these helpers when there was an infraction of the rules or when tragedy struck…. The employees and trustees of the Home bore the blunt of these tragedies." Henry noted: "It must be remembered that there has always been two sides to the history of these Homes, one good and uplifting, the other sad, bad and vulgar." Henry had also been an inmate at the home as a child.

Anna Lou, Rose and Robert Scholl
April 1928
(Rose Scholl Family)

Former resident James DeWitt shared: "I thought it (the home) was poorly run and I still think it was. They had about 200 acres of land. Course they had truck patches…Garden and potatoes and things like that. They raised most of their vegetables….They never raised their own chickens. You thought they would have. But we never got hardly any meat.

In December 1937, a Miami County Grand Jury accessed the local institutions, including the Welfare Home, and reported: "Is under excellent management and is operating as efficiently as possible considering the buildings they have to work with."

Increasing state regulations led to the home's closing in 1943. The closing prevented an investigation into sexual abuse among the children. A former inmate of the home, on leave from military service, had planned to file a complaint based on personal experiences at the home. Some homes in which the children were placed were also unsuitable, as the foster parents were only looking for inexpensive labor.

This book has a narrow focus on Rose's time at the Welfare Home during 1935 and the children she mentioned during that year. Some of the children had siblings at the home that she never mentioned. In those cases, we provided only a brief mention of those siblings. Rose mentioned several children by only a first name, and some of those remain unknown.

Changes may have been made to some of the direct quotes to clean up punctuation and spelling to improve readability. In a few cases, the original spelling and punctuation have been left.

Eric Flora, October 2019.

Rose Scholl and two of her great grandchildren, Eric Flora and his sister-about 1973
(Rose Scholl Family)

CHAPTER 1: ROSE SCHOLL'S DAY-TO-DAY ACTIVITIES

In the front of her 1937-1941 journal, a gray-eyed, brown-haired thirty-six-year-old Rose mentioned that she and her two children -- Anna Lou and Robert -- lived at her parents during that time frame. She wrote she "had been at Mexico Children home 4 ½ years before." On the first page of her 1935 journal many years afterwards Rose wrote: "Only a part of the work is mentioned in this book that I have done. There are a thousand things in the everyday routine that was useless to mention each day." She received one dollar a day for her work. Rose also listed an additional income of seven hundred thirty-seven dollars from her seventy-acre farm in Carroll County, Indiana. This included revenue from oats, corn, hogs, and sheep. She listed personal and farm expenses of one hundred nineteen dollars through June of the same year. Rose weighed one hundred forty pounds and was a half inch short of five feet five inches.

The ringing of the church and school bells announced New Year's 1935 at the Welfare Home. This year also saw the trampoline, invented by George Nissen and Larry Griswold. Rose started the New Year by cooking for forty-one children during the cook's, Miss Mae's, absence. A Mr. Holman provided the children with five gallons of ice cream for a New Year's celebration.

Born in February 1885 in Indiana, Miss Mae or Nellie Mae Heck was the daughter of Fredrick Heck and Lydia Swihart. She cooked at the home in 1935 and was a cook there in 1940. In April 1938 she cared for her father near Argos before she "returned to her work at the Mexico

School House for the children of the home and the staff's children
(James DeWitt Family)

Welfare Home." Seventy-seven-year-old Nellie died in April 1962 near Argos. She never married and was a member of the Walnut Church of the Brethren.

On the third of January, Rose ironed thirty shirts in the morning and mended so many hose in the afternoon that she "didn't count the number of pairs." The next day, Rose spent all day mending stockings. Dr. Rendel stopped by at suppertime on the fifth. Henry Swayer noted that "Dr. C.F. Rendel served the home untiringly for many years and until he was no longer able to carry on. Dr. Harold Rendel then assumed the responsibility of serving. Both provided excellent service to the Home – often times without pay and then only a token amount."

Dr. Charles Rendel was born in 1875 in Noble County. He married Ruby Agnes Lash in 1905 at Albion. Dr. Charles passed away in 1948 at Mexico, in bed, from a heart attack. Dr. Charles and Ruby had two children: James and Harold.

Dr. Harold Rendel was born in 1917 at Mexico. He married Betty Dilling at Monticello in 1942. He began practicing medicine the same year and retired in 1988. He served as a medical corps officer in the Army during World War II and was a member of the Mexico United Methodist Church. Harold and Betty had four children.

On the sixth, a Sunday, Rose took the girls to church twice, where they listened to Reverend Walter Balsbaugh and Reverend Aukerman preach. Rose dampened and ironed eighteen shirts on the afternoon of January eighth. The next day, she received a card from her mother noting that Anna Lou had come down with the measles. The following day, the men prepared for butchering day. On the eleventh Rose spent the morning cleaning and taking care of five sick children. She worked on a coat for her son, Robert, and sent a package to her children while being "almost sick with a cold."

Mexico Church of the Brethren
(James DeWitt Family)

On the twelfth, Rose spent all afternoon in bed after cleaning the dorm and mopping two other rooms. The next day she and several of the girls spent the day in bed, except for meals. None of the children attended evening church services. After making a dress over, cleaning six rooms, folding clothes, carrying food, and mending eighteen pairs of hose and repairing two ironing cords, on the seventeenth Rose took a "3/4 hour beauty nap." She then worked on a wool skirt for one of the girls. On a damp and gloomy Sunday on the twentieth, she took the girls to church and Sunday School, and they heard Reverend Harley Fisher preach. In the evening they attended the First Brethren Church to hear Evangelist Studebaker. On the twenty-first of January, Rose shared "Did not feel well enough to wash."

M.E. Miller wrote: "The orphans and young people of the Home attended Church and Sunday School regularly, marching along with their caretakers. The young people of the church often invited young people from the Home to have Sunday dinner with them and many of the youth from the Home became members of the church."

After a morning of sewing, mending, and pressing clothes on the twenty-fifth of January, Rose noted "Heard a 'thrilling' talk by a reporter on the Lindberg-Hauptmann case. Richard Bruno H. being cross-examined for 45 minutes. This p.m. in New Jersey-Flemington." In March 1932, a twenty-month-old Charles Lindbergh, Jr. disappeared from his crib in his New Jersey home. They found his body in May. In September 1934, authorities arrested Richard Hauptmann. His trial ended with a death sentence in February 1935.

On the twenty-eighth, they hung clothes outside for "the first for a long time." Henry Swayer shared his memories of wash day. "For the children there were at least 16 of these washers and as many as 20 boys to take turns operating them if the boys could be found. After the clothes were through the wringer, they were taken out to a quarter of an acre of clothes lines and hung up to dry. Try to picture anyone hanging up wet clothes for up to 3 hours in freezing weather today."

C. Henry Swayer was born in 1902 in Montana. In 1910 he lived with his grandparents in Montana. Henry wrote: "I first knew the Home personally in September 1912. In this Home I was first introduced to communal living. Here I made my first childhood friendships, developed my first puppy love, courted my wife while she was working there." Ten years later he lived with the Ralph and Edna Greer family in Jefferson Township, Miami County. He worked for the Wabash Railroad and then operated nursing homes in Indiana and Iowa from 1947 until he retired in 1974. He married Edna Miller in 1924 at Mexico and passed away in 1978 there. Henry and Edna had five children.

The same day, the twenty-eighth, most of the children watched a movie: "Little Minister." The movie, released in 1934, starred Katharine Hepburn and took place in Scotland in the 1840s. On the twenty-ninth, Rose helped take care of five sick children and ironed thirty-three shirts, all of her clothes, and the children's clothes.

On the thirtieth, thirty-nine men showed up to help butcher seventeen hogs. Rose served dinner to all the men while the children ate upstairs. The next day they canned one hundred fourteen quarts of meat. They fried two gallons of side meat and fourteen gallons of sausage. On the first day of February, Rose and Miss Mae worked most of the day with the meat. Rose noted: "We now have 23 gal. and 36 qt. of sausage, 22 qt. liver, 16 gal. side meat, 92 qt. ribs tenderloin and 7 gal. of fried tenderloin. We hardly took time to eat. Then when I came upstairs, I became very sick and could not be with the children at supper but before bedtime I am better. And ate a serving of brains. I think they are such a fine dish."

Thurman Glassburn recalled butchering day: "One thing I'll always remember about the Home was butchering day. Always done in

January and with the help of people from outside the Home. I always got away and turned my back so I would not see the hogs being killed. They had all become our friends because we fed and cared for them."

Henry Swayer shared his memories of butchering day. "This was a day set reasonable in advance, in accordance with expected weather conditions, and I have a feeling according to the sign of the moon. On the morning of the appointed day at 2 a.m. the superintendent or farm manager would light the fires under 6 or 8 kettles of water for scalding hogs....Three scalding barrels were in place beside a platform.... As soon as the sight of a rifle could be seen and the water was right, the shooting started and continued until the last hog had been shot. By this time there were 15 or 20 more men on hand.... By then folks began to come from Flora, Manchester, Wabash, Huntington, Pipe Creek, and Peru. The women were necessary in this work as the men and came along and worked just as hard.... As many as 30 or 40 fat hogs passed the scalding and scraping stands. Often times within an hour after a hog was shot, it had been scalded, scraped, cleaned, dressed and cut in half, carried to the cutting tables, where hams and shoulders were trimmed.

L to R: Main Office, Living Quarters and Boy's Dorm (upstairs);
Kitchen, Dining Room and Girl's Dorm.
(James DeWitt Family)

These trimmings were cut up for sausage and the fat was properly cut up for rendering into lard. By 10 a.m. the large kettles were cleaned, reset and cans of cut up fat were poured into them for rendering. During this time the women were indeed, quite busy in the dry house getting the entrails stripped and getting the casings ready for the sausage. The casings were scraped and rescraped until the most particular person was satisfied, they were perfectly clean enough to be stuffed with sausage…. when the meat was ground it was placed in large tubs. Then some of the strong-armed men would roll their sleeves to their elbows, wash good and get ready to mix sausage. Someone would salt, pepper and add other seasoning to this and then the mixing began. It was mixed until the seasoning was worked through. The meat was then put into the press, which had a metal spout about 9 inches long where the casing would be placed on. Now the fun began! There were usually 6 to 8 of these presses turned by other strong arms…. This was an art. If not properly done the sausage would be irregular in size, anywhere from the size of a pencil to a person's head…. By 3 p.m. the folks began to leave for home…. Everyone had a good time, and much help had been accorded to the Home…. For the superintendent or farm manager, they would wake up the next morning with the knowledge that possibly a ton of pork awaited processing. According to the weather it would have to be processed at once or put off hoping the weather would stay cool enough to keep this meat until it could be properly taken care of."

James DeWitt shared his butchering memories: "The year I took care of the hogs they had 22. It was an interesting day when they butchered. They'd get people from the church. They had it all set up. By nighttime it was all done. Lard was made. They'd shoot the hogs down in the hog pen and have a horse drag them up. They had it set up behind the powerhouse and wash house. They had set up a ramp. They'd pull the hog up on that ramp. The steam room was right there. They'd dump the hog in that hot water….They would scrape the hair off it. A few minutes later it was hanging up…. Somebody would be there cutting the hog. They had cows. 1/3 of milk went to old folks home. They never butchered a steer in my life that I know of there."

On the second day of February the children were well enough for the staff to move the beds out of the sick room to the dorm room. The next day Rose and the girls attended Sunday School and church. She noted "The ground hog did not see his shadow." They then walked to the "Old Home" to view Grandma Sickler, who had died. Martha Stower Sickler was born in 1843 in Michigan to her New York parents, Bartharic Stower and Maria Field. Martha married James Sickler in 1862. James died in 1910. Martha moved to the home in October 1932. Ralph Rarick assisted in the funeral service, and he and his wife sang a duet at the funeral.

After spending the sixth removing clothes from the dryer, ironing and mending hose Rose wrote "I am planning to go home tomorrow. Can hardly wait." On the seventh she left Mexico in mid-afternoon and took the bus to Logansport, where her mother picked her up.

On a rainy and icy eighth day of February Rose had lunch with her brother, Leonard, and his wife. Rose spent the rest of the day doing mending and in the evening the family played games. She noted "Seems so good to be home." On Saturday, Rose and her children drove to Flora and met with Frank Roskuski and her sisters, Edna Dutter and Cordelia Kuns. Rose noted "So we have spent a Saturday strangely scheduled." The same day Rose paid John Leedy two hundred dollars towards her farm loan. In April of the previous year she had paid John seven hundred dollars towards her loan.

On Sunday afternoon, her father, Adam, and her children took her to Rockfield, and she took the bus back to Mexico. She then took the girls to church. On the twelfth, the staff filled the dryer and completed the washing by first recess. They carried dinner over to the school, "which we have about 11:20 during school." Samuel Reed, who lived in the Old Folks Home, once remarked he couldn't enjoy Sunday evening church services for thinking about washing the next day. He told John Appleman "If they wash in Heaven, I don't believe I care to go."

A controversy erupted at the dedication of the school in September 1905. "The complaint was against the manner of conducting the dedication of the schoolhouse at the Orphan's Home, such as instrumental music and a select choir. The Trustees had given Bro. Appleman authority to arrange for the exercise, which he had done without thought of giving offense. All concerned expressed regret that exceptions had been taken. With a very few exceptions, they were fully acquitted. Then a few asked for an admonition, which was given."

On the thirteenth, Rose ironed, sewed, and mended stockings while the children attended a movie to see "Bright Eyes," featuring Shirley Temple. Shirley played an orphan in the first film written and directed specifically for her.

On Valentine's Day evening Rose wrote they "had a birthday and Valentine celebration. Played games, had ice cream, and all seemed to enjoy themselves." On the fifteenth, Rose made cherry dumplings for the children's supper. She noted "And do they eat them? YES." The next day, Rose made three cakes, ten plum pies, and ten shells. They served fried potatoes for dinner and Rose asked, "Can you guess how many potatoes it takes to satisfy 48 people?" After dinner, Rose made noodles and orange jello.

On the seventeenth, Rose did not attend church but stayed at the home and made eight butterscotch pie fillings. After dinner she took a nap and took the girls to evening church services. The next day, Rose helped the girls fill the dryers. She then mopped the kitchen in place of the girls who were sick and prepared dinner. After dinner she took a short nap before hanging the sheets out. Rose spent the morning of February nineteenth emptying dryers, dampening, folding and washing clothes. She noted: "Making steps for sick folks takes one's time".

On Sunday, Rose and the girls attended Sunday School. Rose wrote: "There is preaching only on 1st, 3rd & 5th Sunday." The water pump also quit working, and a Mr. Stoffer repaired it. The men sowed clover seed on February twenty-seventh, and all the children except the "toddlers" went to see a Will Rogers show. The film may have been "The County Chairman," as the studio released it on the eleventh of January 1935. Will died in an Alaskan plane crash the following August. The same evening Rose noted she "stayed up with Kathleen and Elvera 10:30."

On the twenty-eighth, Rose washed, ironed, and mended some of her own clothes. On a "fine" first day of March, Rose made Anna Lou a red dress and a white collar. She noted that the Wards had brought bread to the home. The next day Rose noted: "Such fine weather as we are having. March is coming in as a lamb." They had halibut for supper. On Sunday, Harley Fisher preached on Ananias and Sapphira at morning church services. Rose didn't wash the next day, since she had suffered from "lumbago or something since Saturday."

The next day Rose ironed twenty-four shirts and helped make sandwiches and carry food to the first floor for the Sunday School Class Party. After completing the cleaning on the ninth, Rose noted "I haven't done much else for I've been so disappointed in not hearing from the kiddies that I really have the blues. Feb. 26 is the last line I got from them. And I've just lived from one day to the next in hopes. Now I must wait until Monday." Two days later the card, written eleven days earlier, arrived. Rose noted "The cause of my suspense. Was mislaid by carrier."

After ironing thirty-one shirts on the twelfth of March, Rose made fudge for the sixth grade and younger girls; who did not go with Mrs. Hendrix to see the movie "David Copperfield." Mrs. Hendrix may have been fifty-five-year-old Mary Hendricks. In 1930 Mary, a widow, lived with Harry and Nellie Wilson in Miami County and worked as a housekeeper. Mary died in 1959. Rose also had an address for a Mildred Hendrix Brechbiel of Bunker Hill. Mildred married in 1927, so it seems unlikely Rose would have referred to her by her maiden name. Mildred had a daughter born about 1934 and the chances of her working at the home around that time seem unlikely.

Two days later, there was a conference at the Mexico First Brethren Church. After the conference several ladies from Flora stopped by and visited with Rose. The visitors included Mrs. Cripe, Mrs. Pope, Mrs. Jordan, Mrs. Clara Flora, Edith Ferguson, Mable Flora, and Mary Fisher.

Rev. Ralph G., Kathleen, Evelyn (back), Vinna and Elvera Rarick
1932
(Rose Scholl Family)

After dinner on the sixteenth, almost everyone walked down to the river, and Ralph Rarick and a Mr. Richey planted a tree beside the water fountain. Ralph Rarick took over as Superintendent from Marion Norris in January 1934. He continued in the position until September 1937, when Lawrence Deardorff replaced him as Superintendent. Superintendents were asked to "avoid the excessive use of tobacco, and to only allow smoking in the smoking room" and to "caution all inmates who leave the Home not to talk disrespectfully of the same."

James DeWitt recalled the Rarick's first day at the Welfare Home: "He had the 3 girls lined up in front of him and his wife. He had them standing in front of 21 boys there. And he introduced his family and then made us say our name and our age and started with the tallest on and went down the line. The girls looked like scared rabbits. One of them was fifteen. One was ten. One was five. When he got down the line, there I guess I was kinda moving around this way and I said 'I am Jim DeWitt. I am eleven going on twelve.' And this girl just smiled at me. I tell you it was just like I went on cloud nine. I just fell head over heels in love with that smile." James rarely forgets a date but based on other sources he may have been a year older than he recalled.

Later Elvera Rarick's mother allowed her and James to play games together in the reception room under her supervision. This lasted until Mr. Rarick found out and said: "We are not supposed to fraternize with any of the kids here." Weeks later they placed James with a family a hundred miles away. James believes "with all of his heart" this was the reason they placed him so far away.

After returning home from Sunday School and church on Sunday, March seventeenth, Rose's parents and children were waiting on her. They visited with the "old people during their dinner." That afternoon Rose made two different trips and took the girls for rides. Rose then returned home with her parents for a few days. While at home, she visited with John Leedy and perhaps she made a payment on the farm. At Rossville she and her mother picked up seven hundred chicks. Three days later, Rose returned to the home in the late afternoon. She paid sixty-five cents for the bus trip from Logansport to Mexico.

On the twenty-first, Rose took the girls fishing and noted that they "caught several." The next day, the trustees visited the home.

Henry Swayer wrote: "While most of the men who were elected trustees of the Home were hard-working, dedicated men, there were a few who found the work distasteful, and for reasons of distance could render little service of the home. Many of them went far beyond the call of duty both in work and support of the Home."

A day later, after dinner, fifty-five children and adults from the home traveled to the circus headquarters and spent the afternoon. After dinner Rose took the girls on a three-mile hike. At church in the evening, they listened to Reverend Harley Fisher preach on "Conscience." The trustees were at the Welfare Home on the twenty-fifth of March "to look around." Rose spent the day working on eighty-five yards of curtains while the men planted trees.

Three days later, a fire insurance official inspected the home. In the evening, everyone enjoyed crackerjack, while a "Mr. Holman has come out with a company of people from Peru to show pictures and give their program. The Catholic Priest also gave a talk. A couple from the circus sang." The next day, Rose received a "nice letter" from Anna Lou and Robert and noted that Anna Lou won second place in a Delphi spelling contest.

After completing Saturday's cleaning, they fished at the river. Rose reported that "Lois caught 5. Miss Mae came down and we four, Alberta, Priscilla, Miss Mae & I gathered dandelions. Had a good mess for supper. Also, some '40 fathom' fish." The Bay State Fishing Company of Boston advertised fresh 40 Fathom Haddock fish fillets during this time period. On a cool last day of March, Rose and the girls attended church where eighty-five-year-old Mr. Holsinger preached. In the evening, they listened to L. Yarner preach.

Men removed the old plaster from the boy's hall on the first of April. The next day, the high school girls attended a high school play titled "Elmer." On the third, after removing clothes from the dryer, Rose noted "Then I went to bed. Didn't go to sleep last night until after

2:30. I doctored all night. Such a cold on my lungs. Have been in bed all afternoon. Such a headache tonight."

By the next day, Rose was feeling better, and she received a card from John Leedy. On the sixth, she spent much of the day cooking. "Made 16 pies, 6 shells, 3 cakes and after dinner I made a batch of noodles and made Cracker Jack for girls & boys using 18 cups of sugar and 9 of sorghum. Made a gallon of jello since supper." On Sunday, Rose made meat loaf from eighteen pounds of hamburger. She also made butterscotch pudding and pineapple salad.

On a cloudy and damp eighth day of April, Rose noted: "I slept over time this morning. 5:20 when I awoke and did I scamper. I made biscuits for the kiddie's dinner using 25 cups of flour. Not a one left. Made 3 peanut butter pies and this p.m. made 11 dishes of butterscotch pudding. For I generally plan something for suppers even if we expect Miss Mae at 2:45. Made a big pan of Spanish noodles for dinner & they are gone. Plasterers were here for dinner." Two days later, Rose and Miss Mae picked dandelions by the "Old Mill."

The plasterers spent the day patching holes, and most of the kids enjoyed watching "Little Colonel" featuring Shirley Temple. The movie had the "first interracial dance pairing in Hollywood history and was so controversial that they cut out the scene in the south." The tap dance featured Shirley and Bill Robinson.

They walked down to the river on the thirteenth, but it was "too swift and high to fish," so they "gathered a big pail of greens." The next day, after attending Sunday School, they enjoyed an Easter Cantata.

Two days later, a snowy day, Rose had a "catch in my back" and "are not doing much" other than some sewing. She noted it was cold enough that the children requested that the stove be put back up. "Put the stove up again today-is so cold-Tulley's remark." They had removed the stove two days earlier. During a cold spell during the winter of 1915-16, the heating system froze, and Henry Swayer noted ".... it was nothing to hear children crying with cold even though they had all their clothing on and wrapped in covers."

After cutting hair the next day, Rose sewed and ironed fifteen shirts. By late evening, she noted: "Am ready for bed at 10. My back is no better. Didn't feel able to do our washing yet." After taking a thirty-minute nap after dinner the next day, Rose noted: "Tonight 5 of Elvera's guests were to a birthday supper. Had fish, goodies as ice cream, cake. The children all had ice cream tonight. Took the children to the Passion Picture at the church."

Rose, on the eighteenth, helped cut up fifty-four quarts of beef. After doing the Saturday cleaning two days later, Rose took the girls fishing in the afternoon. That evening they celebrated with popcorn. After dinner on the twenty-third, Rose took the girls fishing. She worked on a shirt for her son Robert "while sitting along the 'banks of the Eel.'" She then took the high school girls to commencement, where J.O. Winger spoke. On the evening of the twenty-fourth, Rose took the girls to see a magician.

The next day Rose left for a weekend trip to Michigan with friends. They visited Lansing, Eaton Rapids, and Potters Park. They came through Battle Creek and Kalamazoo on the way home. They had a flat tire at Lake Manitou that a Doctor Babcock changed.

On the twenty-ninth, Rose took the girls fishing and violet hunting. The next day, a cool one with the apple trees blooming, Rose and the girls caught a dozen small fish. On the third of May, Rose's sister, Cordelia, and her husband Evert Kuns, brought June and Phyllis back along with Rose's children. Anna Lou walked into town and bought candy for the girls. The next day, the water pump stopped working, and they had no hot or cold water so they could not clean until evening. Rose noted that five men were putting down new linoleum in the bathroom and the boy's washroom.

After attending both morning and evening church services on the fifth, Rose noted "The girls have been taking sick spells for the last few days. Don't know reason." On the tenth, Rose noted they sold two hundred bushels of potatoes.

The next day, after cleaning, Rose "took a rest since dinner." She noted she declined to go mushroom hunting with the girls, and the men finished painting in the 'big boys' dorm.' On Mother's Day, Rose's brother, Leonard, brought Anna Lou and Robert up for a week's visit. She reimbursed Leonard one dollar. The home had a hundred visitors in the afternoon from the Church of the Brethren's Young People's Convention. In the evening, everyone went to church and enjoyed "another play and a talk by an Indian."

Robert and Anna Lou Scholl "on Welfare Home Lawn Mexico, Ind."
(Rose Scholl Family)

Rose, on the thirteenth, "Took the children for an outing this p.m." On a cold and cloudy fifteenth, the men planted fruit trees, and Rose and Anna Lou sewed. Rose noted: "Robert is by my side constantly." After cutting Robert's hair and doing some sewing on the sixteenth, Rose wrote: "The week is just flying. The children think so too. They have been playing some games." Two days later, a Mr. Burrows put a new floor in the playroom. On Sunday, Rose's parents and her brother Joe came up and took Anna Lou and Robert back home. Rose wrote: "Had 6 rabbits for dinner. Anna Lou went to S.S. & church with the girls. I made 12 pies, pineapple salad, butterscotch pudding, shrimp salad, etc. for dinner. Robert stayed with me since dinner. Took some pictures."

On the twentieth, Rose made a birthday cake for a Kathleen and "a lot of noodles" while the girls hung up clothes. After doing the washing, they made four gallons of ice cream. Rose noted: "Got up at 4:30. So am eager to get to bed. But the girls wanted to play 3 deep awhile." The game requires a large group of people who receive slips of paper containing a word. You have to find the two other people with a word associated with your word. They designate each word as the bottom, middle, or top. Once you find the two other people, you have to set on each other's laps in the proper order. On the twenty-first, the girls hung out the clothes and did the ironing on a very "nice" day. Rose noted she made biscuits for supper and used thirty-five cups of flour. She noted "5 biscuits were left. None for first-floor table."

Two days later, a Mr. Burrows applied another layer of varnish to the playroom floor. The next day was such a "nice day" that the girls washed the windows and the woodwork while Rose "shrunk 8 spreads. Mended a lot of bloomers. Made 2 blinds for playroom windows." On the twenty-seventh after hanging out clothes and then ironing them, Rose took the girls swimming at the river. She noted "They enjoyed it."

The next day, Rose noted: "A wreck happened here in the yard since supper. No one injured. A car smashed and Mr. Rarick's lawn ruined. Quite a crowd has gathered. Are still around at 8 o'clock." The next afternoon the girls watched the movie "Our Little Girl" with Shirley Temple. This was one of the few films in which Shirley didn't play an orphan. She also did no dancing, and she only sang a single song in the film. On the thirtieth, Mr. and Mrs. Rarick took the little boys to a parade, and the older boys attended in the evening.

Afterwards everyone walked to the river and swam. Rose noted "I've not been in yet."

On the last day of May, Rose spent the day sewing and helping the girls with their dresses. On the first of June, Mr. and Mrs. Rarick brought a Victrola for the boys.

The next day, a rainy one, Rose noted "We were to church this morning. Reverend Walter Balsbaugh preached. Text 'Opportunity'.... This evening we went to church. L. Aukerman preached. 'Salvation' was text. Sundays are nearly always the same here – don't really have a chance for a well-earned nap." On the fourth, seven of the boys and girls attended a class party at Logansport, and five of the boys watched a ball game.

Two days later, Rose and Myrtle retrieved the summer dresses from the attic while Roland took five boys to a ball game at Wabash. On the morning of the seventh, Rose turned sixty yards of muslin into sheets. In mid-afternoon she took the bus home, and her father and children picked her up. Rose noted they "had a fine fish supper" and afterwards went to Henry Skiles for strawberries. Rose spent much of her vacation at the Old German Baptist Annual Meeting at Rossville on the Daniel Skiles farm. On the thirteenth Rose returned to Mexico on a slow bus. "New motor causes slow driving. Are holding Mexico bus for me. Got there at 5:35." The bus trip cost her one dollar sixty cents.

The next day, Rose took the girls swimming but noted "as of yet I have not gone in." She described the following Sunday: "We went to S.S. and church. Lillian Grisso gave a talk. After dinner I took the girls for a walk. Just got back when a hard shower was on hand. Went to Greenlawn Cemetery and to dam to watch swimmers. This evening we went to children's day exercise at First Brethren Church." Lillian Grisso was a Church of the Brethren Missionary in Africa.

Rose, on the seventeenth, declared "I'm tired enough to retire. This morning we hung the clothes on the line....We all sewed and braided stockings for rug. Since dinner I made fire and got wash water on. Then we went to the river. Came home and did our washing. Since supper took clothes off the line almost as wet as they were this morning. We got thru washing at 8:15."

On a rainy eighteenth day of June, the children watched Joe E. Brown in the baseball movie "Alibi Ike." Two days later, Rose took the girls fishing, and they came home with five fish. After sewing on a rug and mending a dress on the twenty-first, Rose took the girls for a walk.

Robert and Anna Lou Scholl
May 19, 1935
(Rose Scholl Family)

Rose took the girls fishing again the next day. They caught ten small fish. On the twenty-fifth, a Reverend Canfield from Plymouth "gave some music for children and old people at Old Home." Three days later, Rose received news that her ex-husband, Forrest, was in a vehicle accident at Minot, North Dakota. The next day, a warm one, Rose made nine pie shells, three filled pies, and five large cakes. The following day she made enough butterscotch filling for ten pies. On a warm first day of July, Rose and the girls planned to go fishing, but they ended up canning fifty-two quarts of mulberries and rhubarb.

The following day Rose took the girls fishing and noted "caught a few fish." The same day, Rose received notice that her ex-husband might not survive his car accident. On the third of July, Harley Fisher provided chickens for a feast on the fourth. Rose spent the afternoon making eight pairs of bloomers and a dress and reimbursed Mrs. Rarick fifty cents for her telephone bill.

On the fourth of July, the children enjoyed the chickens and the boys picked one hundred ninety-five quarts of raspberries at the Taggarts. Rose helped can one hundred sixteen quarts and eleven pints of jam. Rose noted: "I came up and laid down. Nearly smothered -- 112° in the kitchen. Evelyn brot me some ice cream. We then had fireworks on the garden hill." Rose also noted she didn't plan to go to North Dakota to visit her ex-husband: "I called Cordelia last night at 10 p.m. and gave up going to N.D. I wouldn't enjoy the trip if I was causing someone a disappointment. And I am so used to them in my life."

Two days later they canned sixty quarts of strawberries. On a cool seventh day of July, Rose and the children attended Sunday School and church. In the morning, Mr. Rarick talked on "Prayer Veil" and in the evening Reverend Walter Balsbaugh preached on "Riches and Poverty." The next day, Rose took the girls fishing, and they caught sixteen small fish. After supper she ironed twenty- three shirts and other clothes. The next day, Rose again took the girls fishing, and they caught seventeen small fish. Afterwards she supervised the washing, since she had a "terrible headache" and couldn't help. The children played ball after supper.

Names and Date Unknown
(Rose Scholl Family)

On the tenth, Rose and Miss Mae canned forty-three quarts of mulberries. In the evening the girls enjoyed an accordion concert at the high school. On a warm eleventh day of July, Rose took the girls swimming and noted "I haven't been in yet." Four days later, they canned twenty quarts of mulberries and four quarts of rhubarb. In the evening, Rose "oversaw a ballgame between boys and girls." After dinner on the sixteenth Rose took the girls to the river. The older children watched "Comic Nitwits" that evening.

Rose, on the seventeenth, took six of the girls swimming after dinner and noted "Only have 12 girls now and 24 boys." The next day the children played ball again in the evening. Rose wrote "I took my fancy work out and 'Watched.'" She had spent much of the morning helping can fifty-two quarts of mulberries.

On the nineteenth, Rose swam with the girls for the first time. The children had another ballgame in the evening. Rose noted "We must be out there when boys and girls play together." The next day the girls watched the boys swim, and in the afternoon, they made four gallons of ice cream. After supper Rose took the girls to the boys' play-room, and they all played games while they enjoyed eating popcorn and crackerjack.

On the first of August, Rose prepared to head home for a few days, on the first of August. She wrote: "Seems so long since I have been there." The next morning, she left on the bus and was in Logansport three and three quarters of an hour later. Her brother, Leonard, and Anna Lou and Robert picked her up. On the third, while at home, Rose, Ruth Brovont, Orvetta Blocher, and Rose's mother helped cook for the threshers.

On Sunday August fourth, Rose attended church and then had dinner at her parents. After dinner she visited with her sister Malinda Brown, and her brothers Leonard and Floyd were there to enjoy ice cream. Rose and Anna Lou then stopped by Leonard's for a visit. When she got back to her parents, her sisters Cordelia Kuns, Clara Yost, and Edna Dutter were there.

Rose and her sisters and a sister-in-law again helped cook for the threshers, and Rose fried four chickens on a warm August fifth day. The next day she noted that the girls and Miss Mae had canned sixty quarts of strawberries and one hundred fourteen quarts of cherries during her absence.

On her first full day back on the eighth of August, Rose wrote "mended some bathing suits & coveralls." She noted "We are all get-ting ready to leave for Camp Mack tomorrow. Packed our bundle of blankets, etc., tonight. The children can hardly wait." The Church of the Brethren established Camp Mack in Kosciusko County in 1924.

The next day, Rose reported: "Anna Lou, Robert & I went with Roland & Evelyn. Arrived at Camp about 10:30. Raricks arrive some later and we had dinner after 12. The children enjoyed boating and swimming. There are 60 in our group. We have cabin 'Invincible' during our stay. 15 are occupying it, including Mrs. Hendrix." The next day, Rose had three boat rides and noted "the rest had more than that." On Sunday they had church services at Becker Lodge and served seventy-two for dinner. They took group pictures and left at three in the afternoon.

On the twelfth, Rose ironed thirty-three shirts while the girls ironed towels and pillow slips. She noted: "Am so tired am going to bed early." On a "very warm" thirteenth day of August, they canned six quarts of cucumbers. The next day Rose noted she was "sick with a cold. Did not eat any supper." Seventy-eight quarts of beets were canned on the fourteenth. She noted her son, Robert, slept all afternoon, and he was "getting tired of loafing." On the sixteenth, Rose lamented that her children would soon return home to Camden. "Have enjoyed the children's visit so much. Am sorry that it soon will end."

The next day Rose baked eleven dozen "overnight cookies," a spice cake, and pie shells. A day later, Rose's parents and her Uncle Dan Wises came to pick up her children, Robert and Anna Lou. She made fifteen banana pies in the morning and prepared dinner. Later she noted "Tonight it's lonesome. Been with kiddies for 17 days." On the nineteenth Rose baked biscuits and fried potatoes for dinner and canned six quarts of pickles in the evening. On the following day they had canned seventy-two quarts of tomatoes by mid-morning. Rose noted: "The girls are sewing at their school dresses. Looks like a dress shop. So many dresses in the making."

On the twenty-first, Rose prepared two bushels of sweet corn for dinner. They didn't eat it all, so she "dried quite a bit of it." Two days later, Rose helped the girls sew on their dresses. In the afternoon they canned fourteen quarts of pickles and thirty-seven quarts of tomatoes. On the twenty-fourth, Rose traveled home for a surprise weekend. On Sunday evening, Rose took the girls to church where Reverend

Ackerman preached. The boys and girls then went to a "pitch-in-supper" at Pipe Creek Church.

After dinner on the twenty-sixth, Rose helped can sixty quarts of tomatoes and fifteen quarts of pickles. That evening she played anagrams with the girls. On the twenty-sixth and twenty-seventh, Mrs. Rarick took all the boys to the dentist. The next day Rose helped can sixty-five quarts of green plums. On the twenty-ninth, they canned two hundred seventy-nine quarts of dill, curry, and sweet pickles and tomatoes.

After hearing Reverend Frank Fisher preach at morning church services on the first of September, Rose's two sisters, Edna and Cordelia and their husbands visited her. Henry Swayer described Frank Fisher as "The Pillar" of the home after the death of Levi Miller and his sons, Isaiah and Joseph. He further described Frank as "a big man, not so large of stature; however, he was well built-broad shoulders, stocky and when he walked there was a spring in his step. He walked with purpose and dignity. As he advanced in years, he ascended to the highest office his Church had to give, Moderator of the Annual Meeting. He developed an executive air that he carried to the end."

On a rainy second day of September, Rose noted "53 are in school counting superintendent & helps children (7 of them)." She spent the rest of the day making three sweaters for the girls and a shirt for her son Robert. She didn't finish until ten p.m. On the third, after working on laundry, Rose helped process three bushels of apples. Mr. Rarick ran the peeler and they canned sixty-seven quarts. The fourth was another busy day as Rose and Miss Mae peeled and canned one hundred six quarts of tomatoes. Rose noted "And so so tired."

Rose, on the sixth, noted "Got nine bushels of tomatoes ready for canning and at 2 p.m. had 110 qt. of tomatoes and 14 of pickles. Came upstairs washed the boys. Put clean clothes on them and put them to bed.... I made Anna Lou a dress this evening." Two days later, after attending Sunday School and eating a "creamy chicken dinner," Rose's children and her sister Cordelia and her husband Evert came up for the afternoon. Rose gave Robert a shirt and Anna Lou a dress. Rose noted "Did not go to church tonight. Had singing at first floor."

On the ninth Rose recounted her day. "Hung boy's attic full of clothes. I mended clothes at noon. Sun was out so hung rest of clothes on line. Done most of it myself…. About 3:30 began washing. Myrtle helped me. Girls got in clothes, scrubbed laundry room and did not quite get thru when supper bell rang…." The next day Rose helped can eighty-five quarts of tomatoes and twenty quarts of pickles by mid-afternoon.

The next day on the eleventh they washed and canned two bushels of pickles and canned sixty-four quarts. Rose noted "Now have 1,480 qt. this season." On the twelfth Rose lamented missing out on joining all of her siblings at a sixty-second birthday party for her father, Adam. The following day Rose wrote: "Until 1 p.m. we had 95 qts. of tomatoes canned. Then canned 14 qts. of Pickles and began stringing beans. Got 5 bu. of Mr. Keyes for $1.00 per bushel. At 4:35 had 58 qt. cooking. The rest are ready to can in the morning." On the fourteenth, Rose and Miss Mae canned fifty-six quarts of beans. In the evening, "the boys popped corn for all."

On Sunday the fifteenth of September, Rose and the children attended church and listened to Reverend Walter Balsbaugh preach on "Every Member Church." At the evening service Mr. Rarick spoke from the book of Esther. On the sixteenth they canned fifty-eight quarts of string beans and prepared another fifty-eight quarts for canning the next day. The next day, Rose reported on her busy day "This morning before breakfast got 58 qt. of beans on to cook. Then came upstairs and did some ironing. After dinner started the washing about half thru and our 20 bu. of peaches came. $1.19 per bu. Left washing and began peeling and canning. Got thru at 8:45 and 115 qt. cold packed." The eighteenth was another busy day. "Up at 4:15. Began peeling peaches at once. We cold packed all but 7 qt. Finish the last canning at 8:15. Got 219 qt. today. 9 bu. tomatoes came in today. So tomorrow its catsup. Have now 2,106 qt. of things put up this summer. Took a bath before retiring."

On the nineteenth they processed eleven bushels of beans and canned thirty-six quarts and made forty-two quarts of catsup. Rose noted "It has been so warm in the kitchen especially." The next day Rose shared: "Washed packed and had 36 qt. of beans on before breakfast. Have been cold packing and stringing beans all day. Canned 148 qt. yesterday. Since supper the girls have gone to the high school to see the pictures Mr. Holman is showing. Boys & men have been cutting corn." The next morning, by four thirty in the morning Rose was washing beans and preparing fifty-six quarts for canning. The men spent the day filling the silo. In the evening Rose took the girls over to the schoolhouse for "stunts and games."

All the girls, except the three smallest ones, watched the Will Rogers movie "Steamboat around the Bend" on the twenty-fourth. The movie was released after Will's death in an August 1935 plane crash. Rose noted they had eleven bushels of tomatoes to make into catsup the next day. She was in the kitchen at five in the morning and helped make fifty quarts of catsup. Rose noted "I am so tired. Took a good bath before supper. Dressed for bed but sat on the floor and talked with girls until 9:15." On the twenty-sixth, Rose and Miss Mae took five bushels of apples and turned them into one hundred twenty-five quarts of apple sauce.

By the twenty-seventh they had turned the heat on in the building, and Rose noted that she "Made over about a dozen slips (outing) and cut out 12 pairs of bloomers and cut out some pajamas." The next day, after finishing the cleaning, she spent much of the day sewing for herself. She noted: "The little tots went into Peru at 9:30 a.m. to see Mickey Mouse at the Roxy."

On the first of October, Rose spent much of the day ironing. She helped stem four bushels of grapes and noted they had also received four bushels of peaches. The second was a busy day. They canned nineteen quarts of grape juice and thirty-one quarts of grape pulp along with two hundred eighty-two glasses of jelly. They then canned thirty-two quarts of peaches. Canning continued on the third with seventy quarts of jelly and honey. Rose noted: "We now have put up 2,820 qt. of food stuffs this season." By late fall, Rose noted they had canned over three thousand quarts for the year.

Rose made three large cakes, fourteen pie crusts, thirteen apple pies, noodles, rice pudding, and candy on the fifth. The next day, she made fourteen banana pies. On the seventh, Rose made two hundred twenty biscuits for dinner and later made twelve dishes of butterscotch pudding. She also reimbursed Mrs. Rarick twenty cents for sugar. On the ninth of October, the state inspector Mrs. Hill came, and Rose noted "she bragged on this division." The next day, Rose and Miss Mae made twenty-four gallons of kraut. Rose headed home in the late afternoon for communion services at her church. She returned on the fourteenth. After dinner on the sixteenth, Rose helped make six bushels of cabbage into seventeen gallons of kraut. Rose's parents dropped Robert and Anna Lou off the next day. In the evening, a group of twenty-one walked to the river and roasted hot dogs over a campfire. Rose's children left the next day. Rose noted: "We have had a nice visit. They had to take turns setting on my lap." On the nineteenth, the little girls attended a Halloween party and Rose helped make four gallons of ice cream.

James DeWitt shared an incident at the only party he could recall at the home. "The only time we had a party was a Halloween party the last year I was there. I was talking to a guy by the name of Walter

Rich. It was in the dining room. The girls were over on their side and the boys on our side. Some lady come over. I had never saw her. She looked about young as some of the girls there…. She told me she saw me throw that rope down and told me to pick it up. (The caretaker) heard it and he come over. And she said 'He won't pick it up. I told him to pick it up.' I said: 'Yes you did. If you ask me to pick it up, I'd pick it up. But if she told me to pick it up because I threw it down, I wouldn't pick it up because I didn't throw it down'…. Right away he tore into me. I didn't know what he was going to do. He had me by the head. But he had one of his hands down here and I got ahold of his thumb and I bent it back. And he let go of it. But he marched me out of there. Got me by the back of the shirt and marched me… to the superintendent's office. Rarick wasn't there. So, we waited and waited and waited. He talked to me about what he was going to do. He was going to send me to Whites Institute. I said, 'I never did anything.' I said 'if you sent me it would be for the wrong reason'…. I don't know what she saw. I don't know whether I was using my hands when I was talking. I am convinced she was honest; it wasn't that. Well, then he made me go to bed because the superintendent didn't come. So, I never got to go back to the party. The next morning, they found out what happened, but they never apologized for it."

On the twenty-third, Rose and others ironed one hundred eighty-two shirts. Rose wrote "I am oh so tired but went to church." At church the Wray Sisters sang, and the sermon was "What are we worth?"

Three days later, Lawrence Deardorff and the boys picked fifty bushels of apples. Lawrence Roy Deardorff was born in 1903 to Eli Deardorff and Dura Gano. He married Dollie Ockerman in 1924. She was the daughter of Reverend Leslie Ockerman and Effie Fisher. In 1930 the couple lived with her parents on South Union Street in Kokomo. Ralph Rarick resigned in September 1937 to become the pastor at the Syracuse Church of the Brethren. The board appointed Lawrence as superintendent and Dollie as "assistant." Lawrence had been at the home for the previous two years. Previously he and Dollie lived in Kokomo where Lawrence was involved with the YMCA and Boy Scouts. By May 1940 Lawrence and Dollie lived in rural Miami County, and he worked as a salesman. Lawrence was a member of the Lower Deer Creek Church of the Brethren at the time of his death in 1982. Lawrence's senior yearbook shared "Lawrence overcomes all hard lessons, which proves his courage, you see. He spends hours devising plans for advertising, a 'tombstone agent' he'll be." Lawrence and Dollie had two children.

Rose and Miss Mae canned one hundred seventy quarts of kraut on a rainy twenty-eighth day of October. They attended church in the evening and heard about "No room for Jesus," An inventory list from October 1935 showed six cows and fifteen hogs along with an unknown number of horses. Twelve dollars of onions and sixty-five dollars of wheat were also on the list.

Front Building: Main Office and Boy's Dorm; Back Building: Old Folks Home
(James DeWitt Family)

On the first of November, Rose and the children listened to a sermon: "What lack I yet?" On the second, a Saturday, Rose noted: "The boys are hauling gravel & dirt and had a breakdown across the highway – broke a wheel. Had quite an audience out there after we went to church." On a rainy third day of November, Lawrence Deardorff took Rose and some children back to the home after church. The sermon was "Heaven." Rose noted they stayed at church for the baptizing and wrote "20 came forward at the meetings." The same day Rose's parents stopped by to see her on their way back from Goshen. The next day, a rainy one, Rose "kept office this evening" while everyone else attended a communion service. She also noted that Ralph Rarick had had a car wreck in Peru.

On the seventh, Rose made five slips and some bloomers and noted she had "such a terrible cold." After sewing she took a nap while the "3 kiddies took theirs." After sewing and ironing on the thirteenth Rose noted: "I stay near the kiddies while they sleep and managed to get one myself." Afterwards most of the girls enjoyed the movie "Freckles." Tom Brown played an orphan who worked at a lumber camp. The children held a "stunt night" on the sixteenth. They had chili soup for supper, and Rose spent part of the day making fifteen mulberry pies and a triple batch of oatmeal cookies.

Everyone attended Sunday school and church on the seventeenth except Rose and the three small children. Rose noted "I kept them. Had weenies, mashed potatoes, corn (dried) and pickles and pie for dinner." In the evening Rose took the girls to church where Reverend Frank Fisher preached. The next day she made biscuits for everyone and noted "58 of us go to the table now." While preparing dinner on the nineteenth Rose made fourteen cream pies and a "large pan of goulash."

Rose returned home on the twenty-first. Vinna Rarick and Lawrence Deardorff took her to Peru, and she took the bus to Rockfield where her parents picked her up. Her one-way trip cost eighty-five cents. She paid twenty-six cents for the return trip. She spent much of her time at home mopping and sewing.

On the twenty-fifth Rose's parents took her to Logansport shopping. They then drove to Peru, where Rose took the bus to Mexico. On the twenty-seventh a Mr. Pierce from Kokomo came to the Welfare Home and "showed pictures of foreign land (Wales) while Mrs. Rarick served a Thanksgiving dinner provided by the Pipe Creek Church." Henry Swayer wrote: "The children and older folks were always well remembered at Thanksgiving and Christmas time. For many, many years the Pipe Creek Church has furnished the complete Thanksgiving dinner with all the trimmings for the older folks to enjoy, always so much appreciated by all. The Mexico Church were mindful of them at Christmas and provided a bountiful Christmas dinner for all."

After attending church on the first of December, the children enjoyed "sliding on the hill this p.m." In the evening on the fourth of December everyone attended the Peru First Brethren church to hear evangelist Reverend Studebaker of Pittsburgh, Pennsylvania.

In early December a notice would appear in a local paper similar to this one from 1927: "The Mexico Orphan's and Old People's Home Christmas Wants. Seventy-five orphan children at your door, who must depend upon you for their Christmas. For thirty-five years the institution has cared for unfortunate children. Thousands have felt the influence of a Christian Home and are now making good in the great progress of life. A large part of this great uplift to the young lives we are sure was brought about by the heart touches of the Christmas season. This year is no exception. Seventy-five empty hearts who are yearning for your love. Let us express it by the Christmas offerings. We know you will not fail them. Inquiries are already coming in as to the wants...."

They included a Christmas want list from each child. Henry Swayer shared: "During the weeks before Christmas each child was asked what they wanted for Christmas. This was known as the children's want list. On Christmas morning each child would receive this gift, if in reason. If it had not been donated, it was purchased with the money donated. This gift was assured, then in addition, gifts according to what was available, along with lots of candy and fruit. There were always mouth organs, horns and every kind of noise maker the mind can imagine. It was no wonder the help went beside themselves before the day was over, for if the din and noise reached Heaven it would have surely discouraged the angels from returning to earth. It was impossible to hear yourself think."

Henry Swayer recalled memories about Christmas time at the home. "At Christmas time gifts for the children, as well as the older folks, came in from many quarters. However, it was the main street in Peru that supplied the bulk of them. Just think, a gift for each of the 100 to 125 children. The writer can tell you that they most always had three possibly four gifts. There were horns, sleds, tools, etc. for the boys, with dolls, dishes, ribbons for the girls and clothes for all. For many years there would be two or three teams and bobsleds or wagons, depending on the weather, to go to Peru for the whole day to pick up toys, etc. They would usually be loaded as they returned late in the evening to the Home. The stores were generally solicited by four of the trustees and the management."

Rose noted on the fifth that Ruth Deardorff came down with mumps and noted "Poor me" about Christmas time. "Hope I may spend that time at home with Anna Lou and Robert." On the sixth, Rose made five new dresses from old ones she found in the attic. In the evening they heard about "The Cross" at a First Brethren church meeting. After completing the normal Saturday work on the seventh, the girls decorated the home for Christmas.

In 1899, Superintendent Frank Fisher found trouble when he allowed Christmas trees in the home. "He said they had two trees with presents on them for the children, but had no Santa Clause, or nothing foolish, nor any deception about it. The Church has nothing more to ask of him but advises to have no more in the future."

On the eighth, a day described as "visiting day," the children attended church in the evening and Reverend Harley Fisher preached on "Seven Dispensations." Only two parents showed up to visit with their children. James DeWitt shared his memories of visiting day: "The boys building…. There wasn't very much room in there…. The main room was where they had company. They wouldn't let you go out with the company and walk around. Wouldn't let the company take you to eat somewhere. Of course, people didn't eat out much then. If they got company, they had someone sitting in there close to you. They censored the mail going in and out. That tells you a little bit of something don't it."

Rose noted she made a purple wool skirt "for a small girl" on the ninth of December. The next day Rose reported "The usual job of caring for the clothes each week. It's the same routine to travel. Did some of my ironing today also did some sewing. The mumps are still prevalent among the boys."

On the thirteenth, Rose reported on her never-ending sewing duties. "Have been making over dresses and patching. Looks like I would get all done one of these days but guess that day will never be." The next day Rose noted "Sewed & sewed today. This p.m. helped Miss Mae can 40 qt. of meat (beef) and 16 qt. broth…. Sent my pkgs. out today. Have tatted & sewed a lot at night to get thru."

On the twenty-third Rose headed home to Camden for Christmas. The Sunday School at the West Manchester Church of the Brethren donated handkerchiefs as Christmas gifts for the children at the home in 1935. Rose returned to the Welfare Home on the twenty-eighth and noted "I have had a very nice time."

On the seventh of February 1936, Rose spent twenty-five cents on "candy to girls." Five days later she spent one dollar fifty cents for bus fare to Camden and back. On the twenty-fifth, Rose received repayment from Mrs. Rarick for two dollars and fifty cents for twenty-five "comfort batts" and blankets.

On the first of September 1936 a local paper reported: "Mrs. Rose Scholl, of this city, has resigned as supervisor of girls at the Mexico Welfare Home, Mexico, Ind., a post she has had for the last four years, it was announced today." James DeWitt recalled "Miss Rose was the best one of all. She was a sweet woman. She was over the girls. She took a liking to our family. I was in the nursery for a couple of years and for some reason she took a liking to me. She was the only bright spot really." He went on to share "she and Alfa Crumpacker were the girl's caretakers and they were two of the nicest staff there. They always seemed to take an interest in the kids."

Old Folks Home
(James DeWitt Family)

CHAPTER 2: THE CHILDREN

Sharon Linn walked to an area of the Greenlawn Cemetery where the seven small tombstones were lined up in a row. Six-month-old Cecil Bright died in August 1895 and his was the first death at the home. The second stone belonged to five-month-old Robert Wickum who likely died in September 1896, but the tombstone appears to show a date of 1897. Four-year-old Hugh Shees, who died in March 1897, lies beneath the third stone. Three-month-old Golda Leeham died in August 1898 and lies next to her brother, three-month-old Clarence Leeham, who died six days later. Twelve-year-old Cora Friskey is identified as the sixth child to die at the home. She died in June 1899. Three-year-old Gladys G. Conner died in April 1900 and was the seventh child to die at the home.

M.E. Miller shared the beginnings of the home. There has been much said about the history of the Church of the Brethren and her auxiliaries…. Perhaps one of the outstanding questions of the church fifty years ago was the problem of her unfortunate members who had no place to spend their declining years other than being thrown out on the mercy of society and compelled to spend their last days in the county infirmary. Our very gracious Father in Heaven with all His wisdom and mercy looks down upon His people in times of needs and provides a way of relief. This was brought about by the Lord laying the burden upon the heart of one of the wealthy members of the Mexico church in the person of Levi P. Miller. Bro. Miller was a very sympathetic and generous-hearted man. He saw the needs of such a Home and was very much determined to accomplish his goal. In April 1889, Bro. Miller made an appeal to the District Conference…asking the District the privilege of building an

Tombstones for the first seven children to die at the home, Greenlawn Cemetery

Golda Leehman, 4th death at Orphans Home 1899

Old Folks and Orphans Home. His request was granted and accepted by the District.... On September 15, 1889, the home was dedicated to Bro. R.H. Miller.... Since they had their home completed, their next problem was to secure a superintendent to care for the Home and its inmates.... Each applicant was considered very carefully, and after much discussion the board saw some very outstanding qualifications in a young brother and his wife. This young brother who was Frank Fisher was a farmer, schoolteacher, and preacher from White county.... One of the outstanding problems soon discovered was that old people and children were not suitable for living together. Bro. Fisher counseled with Bro. Miller in regards to this problem. After much discussion and thought Bro. Miller, as usual, soon had the solution. He proposed that he would erect another building for the children. Bro. Miller presented his second proposition… in 1892. Bro. Frank was Bro. Miller's spokesman on this occasion. The proposition was that Bro. Miller would erect a building 35 by 54 feet for children and would turn it over to the District free of encumbrance if the District would maintain and support it. This was unusual for one man to be so generous as to make such a donation.... Bro. Miller became very much discouraged by the attitude of the conference. He felt as though his purpose was going to be defeated.... Bro. Miller, in a flash, with his wit and determination said to Bro. Fisher, 'You tell the conference I will build, furnish, and support the home without any expense to the District'.... Upon this statement… the District very reluctantly accepted the plan."

Miller continued "As the time went on this second building was erected but there was something lacking. A home and no children. How were they to get the children? The trustees went out and contacted the various counties, soliciting for their patronage. Trustees came in with encouraging reports but when the day came for children to arrive there was no response. Bro. Fisher caught a new vision and without counseling the trustees he went to the various counties with the following proposition: If you will send us your children we will keep them for three months, if we don't locate them within that time we will keep them at our own expense. Bro. Fisher was somewhat criticized by the trustees for such a movement…. However, to their great surprise the children began coming in and Bro. Fisher, being very alert and thoughtful, began placing children to the extent that his institution, within one year, stood in third place with all competitive homes in the state. The great problem of getting children was solved…. He soon realized that idle children were a hindrance to his work… in 1899 at the Bachelor Run District Conference Bro. Miller submitted his proposition to the District. He said, "I am making a distribution of $1,000.00 to each of my own children and I propose to give $1,000.00 to the District to be used for the purchase of 15 acres of land in order that the orphans might have agricultural training." This was a great asset to the Home inasmuch as it furnished employment for the children….There was more land purchased from the endowment fund that had accumulated. The additional land consisting of ninety acres lying near the Home.

Twenty-some days after the Spanish-American War ended, in late February 1899, a local paper reported: "Three small boys arrived here Friday night from Brookston, Ill., en route to the Dunkard home near Mexico, Miami county. A tag was tied to each giving his name, destination and home. A Dunkard minister was to have met them at the train, but he did not arrive until Saturday morning. The little travelers were at loss what to do until they were taken in charge by Mrs. Case, of the Island View hotel."

When a child arrived at the home, they "must receive a thorough bath, and be given an entire outfit of clothing before it shall be allowed to mingle with the children. Its clothing which it wore and that brought with it must be placed in a box for disinfection and two or three ounces of formaldehyde sprinkled over and through them and left therein for twenty-four hours, when they may be aired for five hours and then used."

The Constitution and By-laws of the Old Folks and Orphans Home described how suitable homes for the children were classified. "A first-class home is a home where the wants of the child can be fully met temporally, mentally and spiritually. This first class home need not be a wealthy home financially, but able to furnish the child with good wholesome food, good comfortable clothing, good educational advantages and above all a good religious influence in the home life with the privilege of attending church and Sunday school regularly."

The trustees described a second-class home as "may not be an ideal home in all the points named in the first-class home and yet a very good home for a second-class child. In this class of home, the neatness about the house is not ideal. The up-to-date methods are wanting in this home in a measure. The intellectual standard of this home is not ideal. It may have all the points of the first-class home, but not as highly developed."

The third-class home was "more of an industrial nature, not up-to-date in many things. No interest in educational lines; music and social developments are neglected. This home is not so deeply spiritual, yet encourage church and Sunday school, but seldom go. This home will suit our third-class child that will not fit in a first class nor a second-class home. This third-class child will possibly make a good laborer. Has no ability for higher developments. Does not take to music or higher education."

The Constitution and By-laws of the Welfare Home said that before placing children in a home the home "must be free from profanity, drunkenness card playing and dancing before an agent should recommend it at all. If these evil things exist in a home making application, turn it down until a reform comes."

The same year, 1928, that Otto Rohwedder invented sliced bread, occurred perhaps the darkest day in the Welfare Home's history when three boys, nine-year-old Raymond Todd, a twelve-year-old Derwood Muffley, and fourteen-year-old Bruno Logman drowned in Eel River in July. John Vetter wrote: "On the evening of July 6 the writer accompanied ten of the boys of the Mexico Orphanage to Eel River, adjoining the Home grounds. They all went in bathing and were apparently having a good time. About twenty minutes later the alarm was given that some of them were drifting. Three of the boys got in where the current was too strong and drowned. Soon a large crowd had gathered and searching began, but without avail until the next morning; the first one was found at 5:45 o'clock, the others at 1:55 P.M. and at 2:15 P.M." They buried Raymond and Bruno side by side. Seven months earlier Bruno had asked for an erector set for Christmas.

A small metal grave marker with Raymond's name on it appears in the Old German Baptist Cemetery located at the rear of the Greenlawn Cemetery in Mexico. Bruno's stone is missing but the base remains.

Some time, probably before the drownings, two boys burned to death. In another horrific accident in 1914, the same year as World War I began, William Roberts lost an arm in an engine at the home. He sued the Welfare Home in 1927, seeking ten thousand dollars. William won four thousand five hundred dollars plus reimbursement of his legal fees.

Fifteen-year-old Welfare Home resident, Harold Sullivan, in April 1938 wrote about "The Founding and Improving of the Mexico Welfare Home" for a high school project. He said: "The buildings were not very large at first, but there has been a big addition since the beginning. The wash house has been rebuilt. The hospital has been rebuilt and additional rooms have been added. It is now the home of Mr. Marion Florey. The other buildings that have been added are a large barn, a hog house, a corn crib, a fuel shed, and a dry house. Under this dry house a furnace room was built. Mr. Rarick beautified the lawns of our home by planting trees and shrubbery. He also made cement walks and erected a flagpole."

James DeWitt recalled the first time they sent him out for a trial period with a family. "I was trying to learn to skate between the Old Folks Home and the Orphanage, there was a little area that was slanted a little bit and I was on roller skates. They called me in there. I didn't know what they wanted. They had this feller; he wasn't very big. His wife wasn't very big either, but she was heavy…. They didn't look like they could ever smile. They said I was going to go with them on a trial. I said, 'for what?' They said to see if they want to keep you or not. I said how about my brothers and sister. The lady said we can't take but one. I said how about school. This was the first of April. They said you passed…. I never got to see my brothers and sister. Or nobody I knew. They sent up and got my stuff. The only thing we owned were our Sunday clothes and shoes. Whatever they put in the cubby hole was what you wore…. They took me out and I'll never forget it. I wandered what in the world is happening to me. They lived almost 100 miles way…. They went by Pierceton. There were some people over there they knew. I remember going in. They sit me right beside the door. … They sat on the sofa…. They went in the kitchen. I'm setting there. I could hear their voices in the distance. I thought 'What in the world is happening to me? What is going to happen to me?' All I can remember is this was the first time I ever heard a clock go tick tock tick tock. I never got over that."

Janet Leedy reported on the experiences of the children. "The older children had chores to do before going to school and additional chores during the summer. Laundry duties were shared. Dirty clothes were placed in bins in the bathroom where the housemother checked them for needed mending."

Henry Swayer wrote "Girls hung clothes on a quarter-acre of lines for three hours, sometimes in freezing weather. Boys folded sheets and carried stacks of sheets and towels to their proper shelves. While the girls helped the cook, the boys fed the animals, milked the cows, and cleaned the stalls. A large vegetable garden provided ample amounts of produce to be canned as well as weeding time for the children." The trustees and superintendent "expected that each and every inmate will exercise in manual labor suited to their ability while at the Home."

Richard Dawes "remembers that he always had enough to eat although there were seldom second helpings. Breakfast was usually oatmeal with milk and sugar and postum to drink." In an interview in 1988, Richard and John Olinger "agreed that pork was the meat most often served with vegetables from the fruit cellar or canned at the home." Sharon Linn recalled hearing a story about a boy who ran away from the home and was later found hiding in the lower part of a nearby outhouse.

Janet Leedy shared the following: "The home had its own grade school and playground. High school students attended the public high school in Mexico. The boys wore pinstriped overalls and the girls wore print dresses and long stockings. In summer, after chores were done, the older children were allowed to fish in the river by the dam or swim below the bridge. An adult was always with them. Dawes (Richard) recalls turning the crank on the ice cream freezer and popping a wash-tub full of popcorn."

Richard may have been Robert Dawes, the son of John Dawes and Emma Bell Koons. John died in 1929. James DeWitt described Richard or Robert as a large boy who didn't have any other siblings at the home.

James described playing football with one of the male caretakers with a temper issue. "He was a big guy. Probably weighed a 190 pounds.

I probably weighed 100. He was carrying the football and I knew the only chance I had was his legs cause if I hit him anywhere else, I would have bounced away like a ball. And I took him down. The boys didn't hardly have any playground. They had 8 clotheslines there for the orphanage for hanging up clothes. He rolled over and as he rolled over, he hit one of those cement posts. I know it hurt him. Boy, I tell you I seen what happened to his face and I got out of there before he could get ahold of me. I didn't know what he might have done but I knew it would have hurt."

Thurman Glassburn recalled life at the home: "I was less than four years old when we six Glassburn children entered the Home. The youngest, my sister, was less than two years of age and we were both placed in the nursery. That was in 1924 when John C. Warstler was the Superintendent. I liked him. When I was older, I helped milk the eight or ten cows that belonged to the Home, and to help drive them through Mexico to and from pastureland south of town. I also helped clean the stables for the cows and two horses. One horse was said to have been more than 20 years old."

Thurman continued: "It was the boys, especially, who helped in the truck patch, planting, weeding, and cultivating. I do not recall that the Old Folks had much responsibility, except for Charley Benjamin. He lived there many years, had only one leg, and was an expert at repairing shoes. The matron was like a mother to us. She helped us mend our own clothes. That is how I learned to operate a treadle sewing machine. There were two cooks, one for the old folks and one for the children. We always thought that the folks got the best food. Breakfast was nearly always some kind of cereal. The boys and girls ate family style at separate tables in the lower floor of the girls' building. Bread and perhaps some other items were delivered to the Home, but many other grocery items were obtained from the McGuire and Keyes stores in Mexico. This was a super job because sometimes the store owner would give me a bar of candy. Then I was really in luxury. We never got candy at the Home except at Easter and Christmas time."

Thurman went on to say "The Home ran on a strict schedule; getting up, eating, doing chores, evening devotions and going to bed. The boys especially hated going to bed when it was still daylight. There were two sleeping rooms or dormitories for the boys, a large room for those under about 12 years and a smaller room for the older boys. It was considered a great advancement to get into the big boys' room. No special places were provided for study, but one could use various rooms in the Home such as the playrooms, the chapel, and rooms for meeting family members or friends.

James DeWitt described day-to-day life at the home. "We didn't have any playground really.... They decided we that should stay out there. Well the only thing out there for shade there were two cottonwood trees. Cottonwood is not a shade tree. They are pretty much straight.... Then we had the schoolhouse.... So, there wasn't hardly a place, but we were supposed to stay out there and only come up once a day. Once in the morning and once in the afternoon. I don't know where they came up with that idea or why they did... as kids we wanted to play with water too. They had this faucet. Her apartment was upstairs....There was a water pump outside. It also was hooked into the power system.....When the pressure went down the pump would come on. If you turned it on it would make loud noises. So, we always hoped to get some water in your tin cans to take back out there and play with. There was clay out there and we would make marbles or anything to play as kids will. She would catch you doing it and she would make us go to bed. Over other reasons too, but that was the big one that summer. I went up to get the water. My turn and when I did it. The darn thing cut in. She could sit up in her chair and look around the tree then and see. She called me up there and I had to go to bed for two weeks.... Was in bed all summer.... About 2/3 of the boys were in there. They would get in pillow fights. Then she would extend it. Spent almost all the summer in bed. Had to get up and dress and go to breakfast. Undress and go back to bed. Got up at lunch and then at night. It was silly things. As far as beating anybody. It's surprising, as long as I was there, I don't remember a fight among those kids that had any danger too it. Nobody picking up a rock or club or anything. The kids got along better than most siblings do. I don't know why. We did have a couple of guys that were bullies."

Thurman Glassburn recalled receiving religious training at the Welfare Home. "That was the main thing. You didn't miss church and Sunday School and you prayed before meals. The children were also led in songs and prayers every night before bed. At church, children sat in special pews located on each side of the pulpit, girls on one side and boys on the other."

A 1989 history of the Mexico Church of the Brethren noted: "Lawrence and Dolly Deardorff were Superintendent and Matron in the mid 30's. There were 75 children and 60 older residents at that time. Dolly recalls that the children would line up each night for medications, bandages, attention, and a little love, before going to bed. Lawrence, Dolly and some of the supervisors had a time each month to play games with the children, popcorn, or make ice cream using ice that the boys had helped to bring from the Eel River. The owners of the Boston Store in Peru… would bring things for the children and help to entertain them."

James DeWitt described one of the boy's female caretakers as having "no compassion for anybody. Just a job." James shared a time when the caretaker tried to force him to eat carrots. "First year after we got out of the nursery we had to sit at a table. Four to a table. She put things on your plate, and you had to eat them. She started to give me carrots, and I didn't want them…. I tried to give them away. Usually you could trade food…. Nobody would take them…. She got a dish, and she got more carrots and took me over to her apartment. She took the strap…. and tied my hands up…. But I just put both hands up here. Then she made me put my hands behind me… then she got that spoon and course it hurt my mouth. I opened my mouth. She pushed it in. But she had to take the spoon out. When she took the spoon out so did the carrots. And I just spit them straight ahead. It scared her and she dropped the dish that had the carrots in it. This made her mad. So, she took me into the bathroom. I knew what she was going to do. I saw her do it to another boy. She had me get down on my knees over the bathtub and the spigots for the hot and cold water were there. She stuck my head under there and held it and turned both of them on the back of my head. Well can you imagine where that water went. It went everywhere…..She got wet and so did I. I never ate the carrots. Then she put me to bed."

The Welfare Home provided a home for approximately one thousand five hundred children from 1889 to 1942. The number of children at the home at any one time varied, with the number reaching as high as 175.

CHAPTER 3: ADA AND LILLIAN BAILEY

Rose first mentioned Ada and Lillian Bailey in early November when she wrote: "Mr. and Mrs. Rarick & Lawrence Deardorff went to investigate the Bailey-Williams case today."

Bessie Huffman and Jesse Bailey married in late October 1906 in Logansport, the same year William Kellogg invented Cornflakes. Bessie and Jesse lived in Cass County with two daughters, Mary Fay and Minnie in 1910. In September 1918, Jesse, a teamster, and Bessie lived at 1401 Chicago Street in Logansport. The following year Charles Strite invented the pop-up toaster, and Ada was born on the twenty-sixth of November in Logansport.

In 1920 Bessie and Jesse lived in Cass County with six children: Fay, Floyd, Estel, Mable, Orville and the youngest, Ada. Lillian Rose or Bessie Lillian was born on the twenty-third of March 1924 at Burnettsville. Lillian's birth certificate used the name Bessie Lillian, while her death certificate used Lillian Rose. Her birth certificate appears to have had "Lillian" added at a later date and in a different handwriting.

Thirty-six-year-old Bessie died in April 1925 in Carroll County from puerperal septicemia, with influenza and a miscarriage contributing to her death. In May 1925, Jesse and his children "moved from the Foley property to the old Doyle farm, near Idaville." The 1930 census showed Ada and Lillian lived in White County with their father, four siblings, Fay, Estel, Mable, and Orville, and a two-year-old niece, Vera Fietz.

Authorities charged forty-eight-year-old Jesse with a "criminal attack" on one of his daughters in July 1931. As a result, White County Judge Ralph McClurg sent three of the children, Lillian, Orville, and Ada, to the Welfare Home at Mexico.

Two months later, Jesse pled guilty in court to first-degree rape. They sentenced the farmer to five to twenty-one years at Michigan City state prison. He received a fine of five hundred dollars and was charged court costs of twenty-one dollars and twenty-five cents. Prison records showed that he smoked cigarettes, did not attend Sunday school, and was not a member of the YMCA. The parole board rejected his parole requests from 1936 to 1942. It wasn't until May 1943 that they recommended Jesse for parole. On the sixteenth of September 1943 he was "released on parole, to report full time." By September 1943, Jessie lived in rural Logansport and listed John Banta as someone who would always know where he was. Sixty-one-year-old Jesse Bailey died a year later in late November.

In 1933, Elizabeth Magic invented the game that eventually became Monopoly, and on the twenty-fourth of October authorities placed Ada and Lillian in the Harvey Crumpacker home one mile south of Camden. Lillian shared a bed with Clevo Williams, and Ada had her own bed in the same room. The Crumpackers received four dollars per week for each of the three girls. The Crumpackers lived in a "farmhouse in good repair, comfortable furnished and housekeeping very good."

Maude Williams described the Crumpackers in her state report: "Foster parents are members of the Church of the Brethren. Girl attends church regularly. Foster mother stated she does not try to thrust their particular religion or the type of dress on girls but tries to throw that type of environment around girl. She is teaching girl to do light work and chores about the home. Girl's conduct is good. Foster parents both interviewed. Both seem very interested in girl. They seem to realize their responsibility in caring for girl in home with their 16-year-old boy. They fully realize the protection they should give both to their son and foster daughter. Foster mother states she never leaves girl in the home alone with her husband and son. Foster mother formerly employed at Mexico Children's Home and states she realizes the responsibility that she has assumed in taking this girl into her home." The Crumpackers belonged to the Old German Baptist Church rather than the Church of the Brethren.

Anna Lou Scholl listed Lillian Bailey as a classmate in the fourth grade during the 1934/1935 school year at Camden. On the seventh of November 1935, Judge Ralph McClurg of White County provided the authority to Lawrence Deardorff to move Ada and Lillian Bailey and Clevo Williams to the Welfare Home. A day later Rose noted that "Mr. and Mrs. Deardorff went after Ada, Lillian & Clevo this p.m."

State Agent Blanche Feely had visited the Crumpacker home prior to the removal and filed a report on the twenty-second of November: "Mr. Hatton states he does not know the cause for removal but understands that Mr. and Mrs. Crumpacker went west to visit Mrs. Crumpacker's relatives for two weeks and left a woman in charge. This woman's husband became ill, and when she went home on account of the illness, she secured someone in the community to take care of the child. When the Crumpackers came home they were surprised to find no one there, and in just a short time after the child was brought home by Mr. Crumpacker the Mexico Children's Home authorities came and arrangements were made for removal at once."

Rose didn't mention either Ada or Lillian much after they came to the home. On the ninth of November, she noted Ada made a set of "outing pajamas." And a month later, Rose cut out a dress for Ada.

A Mrs. Inez I. Adkins on the twenty-sixth of February 1937 signed an agreement to keep Lillian until the twenty-third of March 1942, when Lillian would turn eighteen. Inez agreed to: "maintain and treat her kindly and properly as a member of this family; that he will cause her to attend church and Sunday school regularly; that he will provide for her education in the Public Schools where he resides, causing her to attend such Public Schools in accordance with law, and that he will teach her an occupation that will enable her to become self-supporting. That he will provide said child with sufficient and suitable clothing for weekdays and for attending public worship, and with suitable food and other necessaries in health and in sickness. To guard it against contracting habits of profanity, intoxication and the use of tobacco. That at the expiration of said time he will furnish said child with two good suits of clothes and will pay the child at that time, the sum of Twenty-Five ($25) Dollars, or an equivalent therefore which shall be satisfactory to said child and said Home."

On the second of March 1938, Superintendent Lawrence Deardorff removed Lillian from the home of Mrs. Adkins. "We wish to inform you that we have taken Lillian Bailey a ward of your county from Mrs. Adkins where she was place by this home…. A complaint was made by neighbors and citizens to Mrs. Bauer, Director of Public Welfare in Peru, and on her advice and with her and the Deputy Sheriff in Peru we visited the home yesterday March 1 and decided we should take the child immediately."

Lawrence went on to share that "The home was a very nice home so far as household furnishings are concerned but there was no affection and the girl was contradicted in every statement she made by Mrs. Adkins. Lillian begged to come back but had a fear of this lady who was very commanding and wanted to keep the girl until morning. We decided however that this was not wise. Lillian has repeatedly thanked us for bringing her back and shows a scar where Mrs. Adkins threw a knife at her which Mrs. Adkins very stoutly denies, claiming the knife was just tossed into the sink nearby and Lillian just happened to get in the way. It is unfortunate that we have had sad experience in Lillian's placements as this is the second time, we have had to take her from a home. We feel she is a very nice girl and believe there is a correct home for her. We hope this meets with your approval as we wish to serve your county and your children to the best of our ability and the best interest of the children."

On the ninth of August 1938, Geneva Loughry the Directory of White County Department of Public Welfare wrote to the home: "We have recently received a letter from Jasper County recommending the home of Lawrence Stark and his wife Mary Faye Bailey Stark as a suitable home for Mrs. Stark's sister, Lillian Bailey. We would like to know when Lillian most recently has visited or has seen her sister Mrs. Stark also, we would like to know Lillian's attitude about going to live with her sister. Would the child like to go there to live? We shall greatly appreciate a reply from you concerning this matter."

The home responded to Geneva Loughry on the eleventh of August: "We are in receipt of your letter concerning Lillian Bailey and can give the following information; Lillian has not seen or heard directly from her sister, Mrs. Stark for seven years. She would be very much interested in visiting her sister, and renew their acquaintance, but does not know if she would care to stay there. She expressed herself as caring very little for Mr. Stark, but of course that might be different now, since she is older, and people do change."

On the nineteenth, Mrs. Mary Stark of Rensselaer received a letter stating Lillian "was accepted as a ward of the Department of Public

Welfare" and they could pick up Lillian from the Welfare Home. The Starks received twenty-five cents per day from White County.

A month later, Lillian's brother, Orville, wrote to the home from Headlee about his concerns about Lillian's living with their sister. "Dear People: I am writing to let you know about Lillian in her new home. We were at the Welfare Home yesterday and would liked to have consulted with you, but seeing that you had a contagious disease, we decided we would not bother. I am staying with my sister Mable at present. What I want to tell you about is that I don't think Lillian has a very good home. But I don't want to cause no direct trouble with my sister, so I would be very well pleased if you would investigate the place or have some health officer to do so. But don't let on as though I sent you up there.... Guess I don't have to say much more so will have to say goodbye and good luck. P.S. If you don't care write and let us know and we will prepare and go get her. Sincerely yours."

Orville was born in July 1918 and placed with A.W. Ford in October 1932 at Claypool. He married Norma Jean Klingensmith in August 1941. Norma died in January 1991, and Orville married former Welfare Home resident Thelma Glassburn Huddleston in May 1995. Orville died in December 2003 in Logansport.

In December 1938, Lillian wrote to the Welfare Home from Rensselaer. "I am writing you to see if I could have my clothes. Please send my coats and dresses and sewing and of course my other things. Just because I'm so far away you don't have to forget me. So that means (please) write. I've been thinking I'd write to you when I first left. But I'm just such a poor writer than I never care to write. But I'd take time to write to you anyway. Send a letter when you send my clothes. Tell everybody I said hello! Send my report card. When you see Mr. Homer tell him to write to me. Send clothes before Christmas. I'd love to see you and your family. How is that teaser Lawrence. HA! HA! Tell Herbert Morehouse I said hello! How are all the Children and Miss

Mae and Miss Smith. Please tell Miss Mae to write me. Please send my wine coat and my brown coat. I'll pay for them soon. I'll have to close with lots of love to all. I'm going to get ready for school now. Answer soon. Your friend."

A month after the Bataan Death March began in the Philippines, on the fifteenth of May 1942, Lillian wrote to a Miss Smith at the home. "I have tried getting my birth certificate other places & had no luck would you please send it to me. I would like to have it right away please. It's necessary that I have it real soon. Would you please tell some of the kids I said hello! I'd like to see you again. Really, I would. Yours Sincerely, Lillian."

Twenty-two-year-old Lillian Roselie Kleeberg Staggs married Donald Geise in March 1946 at Fort Wayne. In 1975 and 1976, Lillian Rose used the last name of Brown. Seventy-one-year-old Lillian Rose, divorced, died in August 1995 in Fort Wayne. She was a member of the Prayer Baptist Church. She had five children: Donna Kordes, Patricia Huguenard, Mary Drew, Karen Guynn, and David Geise.

On the tenth of November 1937 they placed Ada in the Porter C. Brown home at 915 East Main Street in Warsaw until she turned nineteen years of age. The Browns paid Ada three dollars a day, and she had to "provide her own clothes and incidentals." The Deardorffs wrote: "Mr. Brown is manager of the Sinclair Oil Company, Bulk station in Warsaw. They have a very fine home, and are highly recommended by Mrs. Nellie Arnold, Director of Public Welfare of Kosciusko County. Of course, there is a thirty-day trial period, but we hope this works out fine for Ada. If it doesn't, we will try another place."

The report continued: "Mrs. Porter C. Brown seemed to be a very motherly woman, having had one child, a daughter, who is in her sophomore year in Manchester College. Mrs. Brown is alone most of the time, as her husband is an agent for the Sinclair Corporation. One could readily see on entering Mrs. Brown's home that it was a clean, well equipped, Christian home. Mrs. Brown also provided a lovely little room for Ada, all her own. The only upstairs bed-room, so Ada's work will be easy for her I believe, no small children, and everything she needs to work with and so handy...."

Ada married James Franklin Cox. In 1939, Ada and James may have lived in Des Moines, Iowa, where James worked as a "cutter." By 1940 twenty-one-year-old James and twenty-year-old Ada lived with his parents in Miami County. Eighty-four-year-old Ada died in February 2004 at Kokomo. She and James had nine children: Thomas, Mike, Jeff, Roger, Richard, Larry, Judy Smith, Sue Beal, and Sharon Smith.

CHAPTER 4: PHYLLIS AND JUNE BOWERS

June received her first mention from Rose on New Year's Day 1935 when Rose noted "June is ill today. Not in school." Phyllis was first mentioned four days later when Rose shared "Annabelle, June, Phyllis, and Myrtle have been in bed today but are up for supper."

Eva June Bowers was born on the third of January 1924 at Huntington to Clarence Otto Bowers, a laborer, and Viola Wike. Phyllis was born on the eighteenth of January 1927 in Huntington. Phyllis was the thirteenth child born to Viola. The family lived at 1631 East State Street in Huntington.

Clarence Otto Bowers was born in June 1882 and married Viola Catherine Wike the day before Christmas 1902 in Huntington. Their wedding announcement described Clarence as "a carpenter by trade and is well and favorably known." The announcement described Ola Wike as "an estimable young lady and will make an excellent helpmate." Morris Michtom created the teddy bear the same year.

Gray-eyed Clarence, in September 1918, worked for the Erie Railroad as a cab carpenter. Three years later in January 1921, Clarence and Viola's fifteen-year-old son, Donald J., died from an "abscess of the front sinus and an infection of the throat."

In 1930, five-year-old June and three-year-old Phyllis lived on State Street in Huntington with their parents and seven siblings. Clarence died on the twenty-ninth of October 1932 at Huntington. He was a house builder and died from acute myocarditis or shock after falling from a barn and breaking a hip. A newspaper obituary showed he "suffered a triple fracture of his left leg." The family held his funeral services at the Church of the Brethren. Eighty-five-year-old Viola Catherine Wike Bowers died on the last day of March 1972 at Fort Wayne.

L to R: Phyllis & June – Houston, Texas
(Marjorie Denton)

On the tenth of February 1935 Rose noted that "June does not feel well." On the last day of February, Rose wrote: "Had to get up several times during this night for Phyllis. I am almost certain that she has whooping cough." On the thirtieth of March, Rose shared "June &

Annabelle went to class today." On April Fool's Day, Rose shared ".... I took an old coat apart. Cleaned and pressed it now at 3:30 it is entirely done-a new jacket... for Phyllis."

On the twenty-fifth of April Rose helped June and Phyllis get ready for a vacation with Rose's sister, Cordelia Kuns, and her husband, Evert. He picked up the girls in the evening and took them back to Carroll County. On the third of May, Evert and Cordelia brought June and Phyllis along with Anna Lou and Robert Scholl back to the Welfare Home. On the first of June Rose "made Phyllis a real silk dress from a discarded one in the attic." Three days later Evert and Cordelia picked up June and Rose noted "So got her clothes ready." A month later Cordelia took June, Rose, Anna Lou, and Robert back to Mexico to the home.

On the ninth of September Rose noted "... cut out and sewed at June's dress. ... Cut out a smock for June since supper. At 10:15 p.m. it is almost finished, and I must get to bed." The next day Rose "finished June's dress and smock." In mid-October Rose remade a dress for June. On the twenty-seventh of October Rose noted "Mrs. Bowers came by but did not get to visit the children." Two weeks before Christmas, Rose made June a wool dress.

On the eighteenth of May 1936 Evert signed an agreement to have June remain with the Kuns family as follows: "This placement is for the summer, 1936. If at the end of the time, and when school begins, if it is desired by Mr. and Mrs. Kuns that June continue on with them and that they will provide her schooling, and if the way is clear for this with Huntington County officials and Mexico Home, then this contract will provide for the usual longer period." Marjorie Denton shared how Phyllis "was in a foster home for a while and they wanted to adopt her, but her mother wouldn't let that happen." Perhaps the same thing occurred with the Kuns and their plan to adopt June.

On the twenty-seventh of May 1936 Rose noted: "I went with Mr. and Mrs. Rarick, Elvera, Marjorie Nice and George to Peru. Met the folks there and we soon started home taking Geo. Bowers to Leonards first, who intends to stay there awhile." George was June and Phyllis' brother. Leonard was Rose's younger brother. By 1940, thirteen-year-old Phyllis and sixteen-year-old June lived on West High Street in Huntington with their mother and three siblings.

Eva June Bowers married James Lee Bauman on the twentieth of July 1946 at Fort Wayne. Eva June Bauman died in Colorado, Texas, on the sixteenth of March 2010. June and James had three children: Vickie, Connie, and Peggy.

Nineteen-year-old Phyllis married Robert A. Denton in May 1946 in Indiana. In 1950 and 1951, Phyllis and Robert lived in Huntington. Three years later they lived in Fort Wayne. Eighty-five-year-old Phyllis J. Denton died on the first of November 2012 in De Lon Springs, Florida. Phyllis and Robert had three children: Ann, Carolyn, and Bob Jr.

CHAPTER 5: MYRTLE CLARK

Rose first mentioned Myrtle on the fifth day of January 1935 when she noted Myrtle and three other girls "have been in bed today but are up for supper." Welfare Home records and a birth certificate show Myrtle Marie Clark was born on the eighteenth of April 1920 at Peru, but her death certificate gives a date of the eighteenth of April 1918. She was the daughter of Fred Clark and Rachel Douglas.

Fred married Rachel in Miami County in April 1905. The same year, Albert Einstein published the *Theory of Relativity*. Fred and Rachel had a daughter -- Geneva Burnett Clark -- born in 1908. In April 1910, Fred, Rachel, and their daughter, Geneva, lived at Peru. Florence Isabelle Clark arrived in August 1910, and Arthur joined the family in January 1914.

In 1920 Fred and Rachel, three children (Geneva, Florence and Arthur), and Rachel's father, Solomon Douglas, lived in a rented home on East Eighth Street in Peru. Fred assembled auto parts at a factory. It is probable that Fred and Rachel separated or divorced about 1923. Arthur Clark arrived at the Welfare Home in mid-June 1923 from Marshall County. The county returned him to his mother at Culver two days before Christmas 1923. Thirteen-year-old Arthur died in 1927 at a Fort Wayne institution of General Peritonitis from acute appendicitis.

Myrtle Marie came to the home on the fifteenth of December 1928. They noted her health as "good."

In 1930 a divorced Fred lodged on West Third Street in Peru, where he worked as a Porter. Rachel's whereabouts in 1930 are unknown. The same year, nine-year-old Myrtle lived at the Mexico Welfare Home.

Fourteen-year-old Myrtle, in 1934, asked for a "Bad Wolf red hat or harp" for Christmas. On the eleventh of January 1935, Rose did her regular morning cleaning and took care of Myrtle and three other sick girls. Three days later, Rose noted that Myrtle was "feeling better this evening." The following day Rose noted "Seems we can't get straightened up from sickness. Annabelle & Myrtle do not feel well yet."

On the eighteenth, Rose didn't feel well and noted that she had made three dresses over for Myrtle and Marjorie; she also said that Myrtle had been in bed most of the week with an earache. On the sixth of February, Myrtle and Rose "mended children's hose." Two and a half weeks later Rose sewed on a blouse for Myrtle. On the eighth of March, Rose washed Myrtle's "rose and brown dress" and made a new dress for her.

On the fourth of April, Rose noted that the doctor had checked the children and found Myrtle and three others positive for whooping cough. In mid-August, Myrtle left the home for a week's vacation with her aunt, a Mrs. Haager. Nine days later she returned. On the ninth of September Myrtle helped Rose do the washing. On the nineteenth of October, Myrtle, Thelma Gorney, and Rose cleaned the attic.

Welfare Home records show that Myrtle left the home on the fourth of December 1937, the same year Frank Whittle and Hans von Ohain invented the jet engine.

In 1940, a Myrtle Clark worked as a "hired girl" in Peru for the Ralph Brown family on Kelly Avenue. On the twenty-sixth of March

1941, Myrtle came back to the home with the approval of the Miami County Department of Public Welfare to stay until she was twenty-one. On the twenty-sixth of April, Myrtle spent time at the Miami County Infirmary. At some point, a note in Myrtle's file showed that she "had been admitted to Fort Wayne State School."

Rachel Douglas Wilson died in 1946, and Fred died in April 1949 at Peru. His obituary listed three children: Florence Martin, Miss Myrtle Clark, and Miss Geneva Clark. By 1947 Myrtle lived at 559 Chili Avenue in Peru.

Myrtle married George J. Kaster in September 1961. George had a daughter, Marilyn, with his previous wife, Bertha. Bertha died in 1944 from cancer. Marilyn's daughter shared how George took Marilyn to bars in Gary and had her dance on tables for money. An aunt from Rensselaer intervened and took Marilyn into her home.

After a Friday night "disturbance" in Winamac in July 1949, George received a fine of twenty-five dollars for "disorderly conduct and public intoxication" charges and received a six-month sentence at the State Prison. In February 1955, George, who ran away from Longcliff Hospital in April 1954, turned up in Carthage, Missouri. Five years later he worked as a "driver" and lived in Logansport.

Myrtle died three days after Christmas 1976, during President Gerald Ford's administration. George died in April 1979 at Logansport.

CHAPTER 6: GENEVA
AND JOHN DEWITT

Rose first mentioned Geneva on a cold and rainy first day of May 1935 when Geneva came back to the home to spend the night with her dying friend, Olivine Parker. Geneva left at nine the next evening. Rose made no other mention of the DeWitts until the twenty-third of August, when she noted that John had his tonsils removed at Dr. Carlson's office.

The DeWitt children came to the home from Newton County on the ninth day of April 1926. The same year Erik Rotheim invented aerosol spray. Their father, John, sent the children to the Welfare Home because of his health issues. Twenty-nine-year-old Fern Lillian, their mother, died on the twenty-fifth of July 1925 in Morocco from tuberculosis. John died from tuberculosis in Denver, Colorado, four days after Christmas in 1928.

John DeWitt and Fern McColly married in August 1916 in Jasper County. The same year a polio epidemic afflicted twenty-seven thousand people and killed over seven thousand in the United States.

Geneva Mae was born in late March 1917 near Fair Oaks. Glenn Edgar was born in mid-April 1918. John Dean was born in April 1920. James Clark was born in late June 1921. John and Fern had two other children. Mildred DeWitt died just shy of ten-months-old from cholera in September 1923. One-year-old Lawson Harold DeWitt died in June 1925 from tuberculosis. Two-year-old Geneva lived in a rented home with her parents and a brother, Glenn, in Jasper County in 1920, where John worked in the timber industry.

In 1927, ten-year-old Geneva asked for a piano for Christmas. Three years later in 1930, a thirteen-year-old Geneva lived at the home in Mexico. On the first of July 1931, Geneva spent two weeks with her Uncle and Aunt, Arthur DeWitt in Grant Park, Illinois. James shared: "Had one Uncle that used to come there.... My sister said he would bring a case of oranges. But we never got the oranges."

Glenn, John and Geneva DeWitt
About 1923
(James DeWitt Family)

On the tenth of November 1932, Geneva ran away and didn't get back to the home until four days before Christmas. James thought that her running away might have had something to do with them trying to cut her red hair. In late June 1933, Geneva had her appendix removed. A year later, they placed her with Mr. and Mrs. Clement Graham at Kewanna.

Eighteen-year-old Geneva married Harold J. McLochlin in September 1935 at Kewanna. Geneva and Harold had a child, Arliss Joan, born in 1936. Geneva lived at 507 Bates Street, Logansport, by February 1937.

Geneva and Harold lived in Rochester by 1940. By December 1949 they had divorced, and she had married Peter "Bing" Marocco, who died in 1963. Geneva then married Ervin "Slim" Messer in October 1964. Seventy-three-year-old Ervin died in 2001 at Butte, Montana, from lung cancer.

Geneva sent candy every year at Christmas to an orphanage in Montana. She had never forgotten how they received candy at Christmas while she and her brothers were at the Welfare Home. Her brother, James, claimed the boys never received candy, but he and another boy did find a lot of candy stashed in the pantry once.

Geneva died in June 2004. Her obituary recalled her "feisty independent spirit" and noted she had worked at the Grand Silver store, cleaned houses, and tended bar. The obituary described her as a "tiny little redhead who loved her Queen Anne cottage and despite being legally blind from macular degeneration, she maintained it beautifully. She traveled independently to Indiana, Billings, Seattle and even Reno, but was always anxious to get back to Butte and her collection of angels and her flower garden."

For Christmas 1927, nine-year-old Glenn wanted a tool chest. In mid-March 1931, Judge George Williams provided approval to the Welfare Home to take Glenn to Riley Hospital for treatment of tuberculosis.

On the first of July 1934, the court sent Glenn to live with his Aunt Stella Dempsey. She could not "discipline or support him," and by mid-August she had returned him to the home. The same year, a sixteen-year-old Glenn asked for a "white shirt, size 15" for Christmas. On the sixteenth of May 1936, they placed Glenn with Mr. and Mrs. H. Beecher Rhodes of Lucerne.

Three months before Germany invaded the Soviet Union, in March 1941, Glenn received a sentence of two to fourteen years for forging a ten dollar and fifty cent check. He also had several other bad checks on him at the time of his arrest. In 1945, Glenn and his wife Dorothy lived at 1407 Wright Street in Logansport.

Glenn died in a truck accident in 1950, the same year Walter Frederick Morrison invented the Frisbee. He suffered from multiple injuries, including a "skull fracture, broken leg, broken ribs, and internal injuries" at Aurora. The truck lost its brakes on a hill and Glenn jumped out before the truck crashed. Glenn had stopped by James' one-pump gas station the same day and told James' there was an issue with his brakes. Glenn was a member of the Brethren Church and died at a hospital in Cincinnati, Ohio. His obituary noted that he and Dorothy had three daughters. Dorothy also had a daughter from a previous relationship.

James was at the Welfare Home from 1926 to early 1934 and from August 1936 thru the summer of 1938. In 1927 six-year-old James asked for a horse and wagon for Christmas. He didn't recall asking for a horse and wagon and thought someone had just made up the list. James didn't get what he asked for and never took part in the Christmas list after that.

A local paper noted "Sometime after 1930, Jim was sent to a farm one hundred miles from the orphanage. He ran away and was picked up by the police while on the way to Warsaw. He was returned to the farm but ran away again, going to Chicago and then the Ozark Mountains. He then hitchhiked to Dallas, Texas and then Illinois and was forced back to the orphanage about 1937. He spent the next year there and graduated from high school. While working on a nearby farm he met his future wife, Mary, who was visiting from Florida. 'It was the first time I had ever felt like a human being,' he said. 'It changed my life completely.'"

In late April 1934, the state placed James with the William Tooley family of Kimmel for a trial stay. In March 1936, a state report showed James was "very nice clean looking boy. Has his room and the house is clean, orderly, and well furnished. The boy is very well dressed.... Mrs. Tooley spoke very highly of James; said they like him very much. Boy said he feels he has a good home."

Nine months later a state report on James noted: "he fits nicely into their home. He is very appreciative. He has a hog.... Just recently Mr. Tooley said in a joking way, "Your vacation will soon be up. You have been here almost a year." The boy said, "I am hoping it will be more than a vacation. That I can make my home here."

James ran away in early July 1936, and the Kosciusko County Sheriff apprehended him the next day. He ran away again in late July 1936 and went to his Uncle Arthur DeWitts in Illinois. His uncle called the sheriff and they returned James to the Tooley home in mid-August. They then returned him to the Welfare Home, where he stayed through the summer of 1938.

Late in 1939, James enlisted in the Navy at Rhode Island. While in the Navy, he unexpectedly met his brother, John, on an island in the Pacific. After joining the Navy, James made several trips back to the Welfare Home and sent cards to boys there during his service. James had a scholarship to Manchester College arranged by a Noble County guardian, but he decided to join the Navy instead.

He ran into fellow Welfare Home resident, Walter Richardson, while in the Navy, some time about 1942. James visited the battleship the USS West Virginia and initially didn't recognize Walter. But James said when Walter smiled, he recognized him right away. Walter and three of his brothers, Robert, Charles, and Lewis arrived at the Welfare

Home in March 1929. They were the sons of Herman Richardson and Edith Mapes.

James witnessed the Pearl Harbor attack. He "was outside of Pearl Harbor on the cargo ship, USS Antares, when the Japanese attacked. Since the Antares was outside the harbor, DeWitt said he and eight other men went up to the bow of the ship to 'watch the dogfight.' By that time the U.S. had its own planes in the air. 'While we were watching, we heard this plane coming really low,' DeWitt said. 'It was a Japanese Zero. By the time we heard him, he was on us. He opened fire, and we hit the deck. He wasn't shooting at us but rather the bridge of the ship.' DeWitt and the rest of the crew were ordered to go below deck and that's the first time DeWitt said he felt uneasy. He knew bombs and torpedoes were raining down above him, but he couldn't see any of it."

Mary Banks was born in September 1925 in Panama City, Florida. After being discharged from the Navy, James hitchhiked to Florida to propose to Mary. When he proposed to her, it was the third time they had seen each other. In late January 1946, she and James married at the First Baptist Church in Panama City. They soon bought a grocery store at Wawaka. They owned a bowling alley and restaurant in Culver for twenty-five years. James and Mary's four children grew up working in at the restaurant and bowling alley. Mary died in October 2005. They had four children: James Jr., Karen Noll, Kathy Patrick, and John. As of October 2019, James lived in Culver.

For Christmas in 1927 seven-year-old John asked for a scooter. John was one of four boys who ran away in September 1934. Sheriff Boyd Peterson picked them up near Logansport and returned them to the Welfare Home. For Christmas 1934, a fourteen-year-old John asked for "high-top leather boots, six 6 1/2" for Christmas.

In May 1936, they placed John with the William Showalter family at Roann. The Showalters returned him to the home in early September 1936. Two weeks later they placed him with the Edward Gallipo family at Macy. In mid-February 1937, John ran away "but reconciliation was made."

James recalled him and John getting in a fight at the home. "When I got out of the nursery, I thought I would have a big brother. My brother was a little more than a year older than me and he wouldn't have anything to do with me. He was going with Thurman and James Glassburn. He didn't want me around. I told him but you're my brother. Well he couldn't help it. It wasn't his fault. I wasn't very big. He was stronger than me and bigger. I tore into him. I took a beating. I remember this Thurman Glassburn was with him…. So, he just got him by the arm and pulled him away. I remember going up against the barn and bawling like the devil. Course my nose was bleeding and had blood all over. I thought I'm never going to ask somebody for something."

John DeWitt
(James DeWitt Family)

John enlisted in the United States Navy in July 1939. He survived the Pearl Harbor attack and left the Navy in April 1942. John married Mary Reed in August 1942. They soon divorced, and he married Betty Riddle in November 1944 at Logansport. From at least 1945 through 1954 John and Betty lived in Logansport, and John worked as a "driver" and a "salesman" during that time frame.

In 1956, John and Betty lived in Logansport, where John worked as a "groundsman." Two years later they lived at 330 Riverview in Logansport, where he worked as a "service man." John died on the sixth of October 2001 in Tennessee. At the time of his death, eighty-one-year-old John was married to Opal Johnson.

John, James and Geneva DeWitt and her husband, Slim Messer-1991
(James DeWitt Family)

CHAPTER 7: LOUISE AND ARTHUR DINGMAN

On the eleventh day of January 1935, Rose noted that "Louise and Arthur Dingman came today." Elizabeth Louise Dingman was born on the seventh of June 1925 in Peru. Arthur Wayne Dingman was born in Fort Wayne on the sixth of December 1926.

Louise and Arthur were the children of Eva Elda Henry. Eva's prison record showed Leonard Dingman was Louise's father and Oscar Dingman was Arthur's father. Leonard and Oscar were cousins. But Louise's birth certificate listed Oscar as her father. Eva married Leonard at Peru in early September 1921, and they divorced in 1923. Oscar Dingman and Eva married in January 1925.

In 1930 four-year-old Louise lived in Lost Creek, Nebraska, with Oscar, Eva, and her three-year-old brother, Arthur. By June 1932 Oscar filed for divorce in Miami County, alleging "Cruel and inhuman treatment." He also sought custody of two-year-old Arthur. Oscar and Eva may have reconciled for a time, but in July 1933 she sued Oscar for divorce and alleged "cruelty and non-support." She also asked for custody of a six-year-old Arthur. The fact that both Oscar and Eva were seeking custody of Arthur, with no mention of Louise, may indicate that Oscar was not Louise's father.

Rose, on the seventeenth of January 1935, "made over a dress of Bertha's for Louise," A week later she made over two more dresses for Louise. On the second day of March, Rose said "I remade one of Bertha's jumpers for Louise." In mid-May, Rose completed another dress for Louise. In mid-June Rose made a new dress for Louise.

On the twenty-fourth of September, Eva Dingman received a six-month sentence at the Department of Correction's Women's Prison for Adultery. Her attorney likely agreed to have her plead guilty to Adultery rather than Prostitution, which carried a longer prison sentence. Brown-haired Eva was born in August 1900 in Missouri. She stood five feet three inches and weighed one hundred twenty-three pounds. Prison records showed "Faint scar 2 ½ in. long across right arm, upper part. Scar across thumb of right hand + ½ in. on knuckle of index finger, right hand."

At the time of her incarceration she said Oscar had left her, and she didn't know his whereabouts. In 1940 Oscar had been unemployed twenty-six weeks out of the last year, but he had worked thirty-two weeks in 1939 for a total income of six hundred forty dollars. Oscar died in June 1989 at Wabash.

Prison records showed Louise and Arthur were in the "Dunkard Orphanage" at Mexico. Eva's father had a third-grade education and her mother had a fourth-grade education. Her mother, Malinda Frantz, practiced "good habits" and had a "Dunkard Church" affiliation, while her father exhibited "poor habits" and had no church affiliation. Eva also attended a Dunkard Church and had a fifth-grade education.

Eva listed a boyfriend, Otis Cox, of Plymouth, who was incarcerated at the state prison in Michigan City for a one-year-sentence for theft. Eva received a discharge from prison in March 1936. She died in June 1979, a member of the Peru Church of Brethren. Her death certificate noted she was a retired employee of the Bearss Hotel.

They placed Arthur and Louise with their grandparents, B. William and Malinda Henry at 286½ East Canal Street in Peru on the second of November 1936. A report noted Arthur suffered with "left leg crippled, cannot step up."

In 1940 a fourteen-year-old Louise Elizabeth Dingman lived with her grandparents, B. William and Malinda Henry, at 274 Ninth Street in Peru. The same year thirteen-year-old Arthur lived at a state institution in Fort Wayne. Twenty-year-old Arthur died from an upper respiratory infection in January 1947 at the State School in Fort Wayne.

Twenty-two-year-old Elizabeth Louise Owens married Verlin Glen Haines in March 1947. Months later, in May 1948, Louise married Freddie Edward Tutorow. Six years later, Louise married Aubert Lee Hunter in Indiana. She showed she had divorced the same year and had a previous marriage. In 1977, Louise married Herbert R. Hoos, Jr.

Louise died in January 2015. She was a member of the Peru Trinity Baptist Church. Her obituary noted "She loved playing games, traveling, singing, eating out with family and friends, and being a clown."

CHAPTER 8: CURTIS ELBURN

Rose only mentioned Curtis once when in late May 1935 she wrote: "Curtis went to Robert Richies." Curtis Thurman Elburn, the son of Henry Elburn and Edith Marie Townsend, joined the world in Cass County on the tenth of August 1919. C.J. Holslag invented the arc welder the same year. Henry and Edith Marie married in April 1913.

Henry and Edith had three children: Lucile, Edna, and Curtis. In 1920, Curtis lived in Cass County with his parents and two older sisters. The same year John Larson invented the lie detector. Their father, thirty-two-year-old farm laborer, Henry, died in January 1921 in Cass County from aortic thrombosis.

After Henry's death, Edith married Henry's brother, Wilbur Elburn in September 1921. They had one child, Charles Wayne Elburn, born in May 1924. Edith later married Henry and Wilbur's half-brother, William Confer, in 1928.

The exact circumstances that led to the children going to the Welfare Home are unknown. Edith had at least eight children with her three husbands. Wilbur and Edith had a son, Wilbur, Jr., born in 1926. In 1933, Wilbur applied for admission to the Indiana Deaf School for Wilbur, Jr. Perhaps Curtis and his sisters had an experience like Wilbur's. In March 1940, the President of the Cass County Orphans' Home Board, Elizabeth Terflinger, described Wilbur Jr. as "a very pathetic, scared and bewildered little boy, so emaciated and under nourished, he seemed only skin and bones. His heart was bad and nothing we did could tempt his appetite…. There seems to be no ties, no loving family interest to ease his future…."

Curtis and his sister, Lucile, came to the home on the twenty-seventh of October 1928 by a judge's order. The home listed their father, Henry, as "dead." On the eleventh of May 1929, they placed Curtis with sixty-two-year-old Samuel Wilson, who lived in Miami County, three and a half miles east of Chili. A state report described Samuel and Cora Wilson as "rather frail at present" and noted that Curtis' mother had not visited him "since last fall." They described Curtis as "seems bright."

Henry, Edith and Lucile Elburn
(Curtis Elburn)

A state report in May noted "county authorities follow boy's apparent stubbornness." Maude Williams said "…. light chores about the house and farm. Conduct good at present. It has seemed a little hard for boy to adjust himself but is showing marked improvement. Does not often show the stubborn disposition he did at first… inclined to feel this might not have been a pure case of stubbornness or sort of a resentful spirit in that he does not like his foster home because Visitor believes he does but because he resents the fact that he cannot live with his own Mother. Boy himself no doubt does not realize just why he feels or acts as he does sometime. There seems to be no reason to believe boy will not outgrow this."

A February 1931 report recommended that "County authorities follow mother trying to visit boy." A teacher, Ernest E. Burch was "encouraged" and said Curtis had "been doing better." Days earlier on the first of February 1931, Curtis' mother, Edith, had visited him. She lived at 130 W. 6th Street in Peru. The state report said "Ernest E. Burch, teacher, stated that at the beginning of the school year boy did not show a good school spirit. Did not know how to play with the boys, was always picking a fight…. Visitor explained to the boy that it is all right for him to take his own part but not until it becomes the last resort but for him never to start a fight."

The report went on to say "On 2-1-31, Mrs. Edith Confer came to the home but boy was out of the house, and Foster Parents thought he had gone to the field to get the cattle but found he was hiding behind the corn crib. Do not understand why he did not come to the house. Visitor asked about this and he stated he did not go to the house because he was not called. Foster Parents do not want these visits and Visitor suggested they take the matter up with county authorities."

A state report in April 1932 on Curtis noted: "Boy has outgrown his suit of clothes and needs new. Foster Mother stated she does not know if they will buy him any clothing now or not." Curtis was getting along well at school but "is giving quite a little difficulty in conduct. Foster Mother told visitor that boy has stolen money from the Sunday school fund. Visitor asked if boy has spending money and Foster

Mother avoided the question but answered that he has 15 cents in his pocket. Finally admitted that he does not have money to spend."

The report said "Foster Father 65, is interested in boy only from standpoint of the work that he can do. Foster Mother, 63, does not want the boy in the home but will hesitate to say so. Inclined to stamp boy as a thief and a bad boy." The report concluded: "The environment is very much against him, and he should have an opportunity to bring out the best that is in him."

During the same time frame, Curtis was in the school play "The Pied Piper of Hamlin" and played the part of Town Crier. The state report noted: "he sings well, and the school is to sing at Teachers Institute 4-9-32. Boy stated he does not know if he can go because he does not know how he can get into Peru."

L to R: Edna, Lucile, and Curtis Elburn
(Curtis Elburn)

On the fourth of September 1933, Curtis returned to the home after the death of Samuel Wilson. They described his initiative as "poor," and he was "careless" in his appearance. They also described him as "stubborn," "shy" but "friendly," and not being truthful. His mother lived at 356 W. 4th Street in Peru during this time. Two days before Christmas, they again placed Curtis with Mrs. Samuel Wilson.

A state report in July 1934 recommended "County authorities make thorough investigation of this home; consider removal of boy." The report said "Boy milks five cows night and morning. Sometimes Foster Mother helps him. He works in the truck patch with a hand plow. Sometimes does not do his work right and Foster Mother has him do it over again which boy resents. Boy feeds two horses and just a very few chickens night and morning. Visitor feels that this is not too much work if the situation were happy…. Goes down to the creek or river two or three times a week to swim. Is saucy to his Foster Mother."

The report went on to say: "is in touch with his Mother…. Foster Mother states that this contact does not do any harm; that the Mother advises him to be a good boy. Stated in the boy's presence that the Mother cannot take him; that she is too poor…. Foster Father Died 9-1-33 and boy was returned to Children's Home 9-4-33 and Foster Mother had her own son and his family come into the home. She only kept him there a month and put him out. She made no complaint of the daughter-in-law or of the grandchildren but did complain a great deal of her son. Stated then that she felt she had to have someone with her and went back to Children's Home 12-22-33 and took Curtis home with her. Visitor feels that since boy is back in this home without the Foster Father, that it is not as good a place for him as it might be. If Foster Mother cannot get along with her own boy, an only child, she may be hard on Curtis. It may be that she is worried over financial circumstances, since she has charge of everything, which makes it harder for her to realize boy's needs. Boy is very sullen with her. Was also sullen with Visitor. Acted as if he were cowed."

On the third of September 1934, Curtis returned to the home as Mrs. Wilson was "unable to give proper discipline." In late September

1934, Curtis, Russell Jameson, James Glassburn, and John DeWitt ran away from the Welfare Home and were picked up by Cass County Sheriff Boyd Peterson on the Onser Keel Farm. At Christmas, a fifteen-year-old Curtis asked for a "flashlight" for Christmas.

A state report in May 1935 noted Curtis' mother lived at 121 South Wayne Street in Peru, and she contacted him on a regular basis by letter. The state agent, M. Maude Williams noted "Boy had gone mushroom hunting and was not seen."

They placed Curtis with Mr. and Mrs. Allen Smith of Wabash County in May 1936. In June, Allen signed an agreement to have Curtis remain with the Smith family until August 1937. By mid-October they had returned him due to "work unsatisfactory." In late February 1937, they placed Curtis at Plymouth with Mr. and Mrs. Frank Wright. They agreed to pay him eighteen dollars a month. Curtis, in April, was returned to the home by the Wrights.

On the last day of May, a report noted "Jess Wilson took Curtis to his home to care for and supervise him in hiring out to work. Because of improper supervision.... Curtis was brought back July 14 and entered in C.C.C. at Lagro, Indiana 7-20-37." The Civilian Conservation Corps was created during the Great Depression to provide jobs creating state parks.

In December 1938, a nineteen-year-old Curtis Elburn lived at Burnettsville, where authorities arrested him and twenty-four-year-old Jess Wilson for the theft of five turkeys from Harley Shaffer. They received thirty days in prison. In 1940, a twenty-year-old Curtis lived with his mother and stepfather, William Confer, in Peru. Curtis had worked as a laborer for forty-six weeks in 1939 for an income of five hundred fifty dollars.

On the twenty-fourth of August 1940 Curtis married Mary Lou Vice at Flora. Both of Curtis' sisters attended the ceremony. The marriage was over by the eighteenth of October. Mary sued for divorce and asked for ten dollars a month and reimbursement of attorney fees. She charged Curtis with "cruelty."

Curtis enlisted in the United States Navy in December 1943 and left the Navy in April 1945. Curtis, a "locomotive fireman," married Betty Fields in February 1953. Curtis and Betty had an infant daughter, Maxine, who died in July 1953. By May 1963 he was married to a Helen. In 1960, Curtis won court approval to stop paying child support as the child was "self-supporting." In March 1968, Curtis filed to run for Second District County Commissioner as a Republican. He came in third place with five hundred nine votes.

In November 1978, Curtis and his Coon dog, Red, won fourth place, and his second dog named Ruby won tenth place in a national field day competition in Cass County. Curtis served as the treasurer of the Cass County Coon Hunters Club and helped hold the 1987 United Kennel Club World Coon Hound Championships in Cass County. Eighty-year-old Curtis died on the twenty-ninth of October 1999 at Peru.

Lucile Romaine, born in September 1915 at Mexico, was placed in late March 1931 with seventy-year-old Viola Workman of Flora. The report recommended that "County authorities follow girl's temper; men roomers." A state report in December 1931 noted "She attends the M.E. Sunday School. Foster Mother states that she had explained to association that she did not send girl to the church of the Brethren because in reaching this church girl would have to pass a pool room and Foster Mother felt this would be an unsatisfactory situation. She usually attends M.E. Church with a neighbor lady. Girl is a member of the young people's organization in this church." Maude Williams then said "Girl displays a great deal of temper which is quickly aroused; however, she does not remain out of patience very long. Her attitude toward discipline is not always the best. She has a very strong desire to get out and work in a restaurant.

Lucile married Jesse Wilson in April 1934. Their son, Darrell, drowned at Lieber State Park in August 1966. Lucile died in August 1975; she was a member of the Miami Baptist Church.

Edna Olive was born on the twenty-fifth of November 1917. In 1930, twelve-year-old Edna lived with her uncle and aunt, Andrew and Elmeda Chambers, on Chili Avenue in Peru. Edna married Robert Dean Looker in January 1938 at Flora. Robert and Edna lived at 207 East Columbia in Flora in 1940. In December 1941, Robert filed for divorce from Edna for alleged "cruel and inhuman treatment.

Thirty-one-year-old Edna Hamilton of 126 East Eighth Street in Logansport married forty-one-year-old Albert Drumm, a Peru truck driver, in August 1949. From at least 1950 through 1957, Edna and Albert lived in Huntington. Edna O. Drumm married Gilbert Cremeans the day before Christmas 1964. Edna Cremeans died in October 1981 at Peru.

Curtis Elburn
(Curtis Elburn)

CHAPTER 9: IRIS FLITCRAFT

Iris received her first mention on the second of January 1935 when Rose wrote: "Iris is ill and not in school." Iris Marie Flitcraft was born on the eleventh of March 1918 in Langlade County, Wisconsin, to Joseph Harthy Flitcraft and Margaret Johnson. By October of the same year, Baltimore and Washington D.C. had experienced so many deaths related to Spanish flu that they ran out of coffins.

In February 1920 the Flitcraft family lived in Langlade County, Wisconsin. Joseph, a sawmill employee, and Margaret had six children in the home: Theodore, Russell, Aaron, Beatrice, Clara Bernice, and Iris. Soon after, Joseph and Margaret and some of their children moved to Peru.

By Christmas 1921, Beatrice, and perhaps another sister lived with their uncle and aunt, Mr. and Mrs. John Flitcraft, at Peru. Russell, seventeen, and Aaron, fifteen, were incarcerated in Waukesha, Wisconsin. Eighteen-year-old Theodore lived with his parents, while Bernice lived in Peru, at Marion Wards, where Margaret worked as a nurse. It is unknown where the other children were at the time.

Christmas Day in 1921 was not a pleasant occasion for the family; Joseph murdered Margaret on Christmas afternoon. One account of the incident shared: "..... While nursing at Ward's home Mrs. Flitcraft did not go home often and her husband begged his wife to spend Christmas at home. She told him she could not promise to do so owing to the illness of her patient. It is said that Flitcraft became angry at her reply and said if she did not come home Christmas, she should not come home at all. Sunday afternoon Mrs. Flitcraft fixed a basketful of presents for her two daughters at John Flitcraft's and some other things for use at home and then called a taxi, in which she went to her home. She told the driver to call for her in a half hour.... The sheriff said Flitcraft asserted that there was no argument with his wife before he struck the fatal blow; that she came home at 3 o'clock with a basket of Christmas gifts for the children and was sitting in a rocking chair in front of the heating stove when he walked behind her, picked up a chunk of coal and struck her over the head with it.... Flitcraft does not seem to worry about what will become of him. He ate heartily last night and again today and slept will during the night."

A second account of the murder shared: ".....Police were dispatched to the Flitcraft home and after digging beneath the house found the body. The woman's hands had been tied behind her back and her skull had been crushed. The only motive for the alleged crime given by Flitcraft in his statement, according to the officials, was that he became angered when his wife did not return home Saturday night. It was later ascertained that Mrs. Flitcraft had been employed as a nurse and had been unable to leave her patient that night...."

Joseph provided a written confession to the murder. "I, Joseph Flitcraft, do herby state that I killed my wife, Margaret Flitcraft, at our home on Wallace Row, Sunday afternoon about the hour of 3 o'clock p.m. the 25th day of December 1921. I further state, that after killing her by hitting her with a lump of coal, I buried her body underneath the dirt beneath the house...."

To prepare for parole hearings Joseph, in October 1937, provided a slightly different account of the incident: "My wife was intimate with another man and wanted to leave me and live with this other man, and hit me over the head with a poker, and I hit her with a lump of coal twice on the head and killed her.... was out of my right mind."

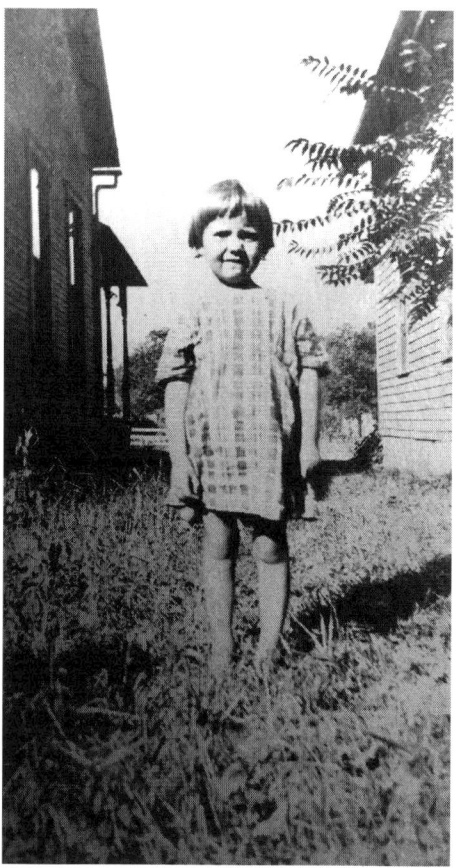

Iris Flitcraft
(Lisa Haughton)

Joseph's sister, Mrs. Levi Starks, provided her opinion of Margaret and defended her brother, Joseph, in 1927. "...He was a good man.... and everyone that knows him knew him to be a hardworking man. Well, his wife was a no-good woman. They moved from here to Peru and there she left her six little children at home with their father while she bummed with other men and wouldn't live with him or stay at home with her children. Now is there any wonder that he done what he did?"

A letter from Joseph's sister, Mrs. Levi Starks, from May 1927 shared: "He has three little girls that need a father's care that are in the orphan's home…." By 1930 twelve-year-old Iris and her fourteen-year-old sister, Clara, lived in Wabash County at Whites Industrial Manual Labor Institute.

Lisa Haughton, Iris' granddaughter, recalled Iris as saying: "I grew up in an orphan's home, so I know what it is like to be beaten." Iris also shared how one of the orphanages she lived at only had one doll, and it was for the youngest girl. Iris had to give the doll up when a younger girl came to the orphanage.

Iris lived at the Mexico Welfare Home by 1935. On the third of January, Rose noted that both Iris and Olivine Parker were on the sick list. The next day both girls spent the day in bed. Iris missed school on the afternoon of the twenty-first of January. Iris again missed school on the eighteenth of February. Both Iris and Olivine missed out on a river walk on the sixteenth of March, likely because of illness.

On the twentieth of April, Rose noted "Iris remade her blue dress." On the first day of May, Rose shared "Iris went to find flour and mended sheets, shirts and spreads." Rose, on the third of June, took Iris to the doctor to "see about her incision." In late July Rose remade one of Iris' dresses for Marjorie. Three days later, Iris and Rose "made goodies to make 2 tubs full of crackerjack."

Iris "mended boy's shirts" on the fourteenth of August. Three days later, Rose noted "Iris has been sick abed today." On the eleventh of September Rose noted: "Iris has been complaining since Monday with her side so had Drs. Rendel & Worl and they took her to the hospital. Operating yet tonight. Came out fine." Two days later Rose commented "Haven't heard from Iris today." On the fifteenth of September, Dollie Deardorff and Evelyn Rarick went to Peru to check on Iris. Four days later, Mrs. Rarick went to Peru to visit Iris. Rose noted that "She was fine." Mrs. Rarick and Dollie Deardorff brought Iris back on the twenty-fifth of September. Rose noted that "She walked around with help." Two days later Rose stated: "Iris is getting along fine. Sets up nearly all the time." On the twenty-ninth of September, a Sunday, Rose shared: "Called the Dr. for Iris. Says she cannot come downstairs yet." Rose wrote, on the first of October that "Iris has had several visitors and they brought her refreshments." Three days later Rose wrote that "Iris started to make herself a collar–is smocking it." The next day, Iris received a new coat.

On the twenty-ninth of October, Rose shared: "Went to church. Iris & Annabelle & Thelma joined." In late November 1935, Iris spent Thanksgiving with relatives. She shared with her family how the children went swimming at the home, and the children were often thrown in the river to learn how to swim. Iris went in after one child who didn't learn fast enough. In June 1937, six of Joseph's children, including Iris, signed a Petition for Clemency. "We, the undersigned parties, unanimously agree that our father has served sufficient time for the crime he has committed. He has now served fifteen years and has an excellent prison record. It is our greatest desire that our father be granted clemency at this time."

At some point Iris lived at Peru with a Shoemaker family. Twenty-year-old Iris married Albert Russell Dale in June 1938 in Indiana. Iris shared how she and Russell often only had an orange or a potato to eat for a meal during the Great Depression.

Joseph died in prison in 1939 from a heart attack. A prisoner, #8032, shared the details of Joseph's death: "I seen Joseph Flitcraft over by his bed and (he) started to leave and walk about 30 ft. He reeled and fell hitting the floor with a thump. We rolled him over opened his shirt and the top buttons on pants and gave him artificial breathing and fanned him; someone sprinkled a little water in his face. He came to a couple of times and moved. Finally, his eyes became glossy and his hand turned white then purple. The Hospital was called at once, and after a matter of a few minutes they arrived and carried Joe out on the stretcher while I assisted them down steps and they took him to Hospital."

Iris and Russell Dale
(Lisa Haughton)

The Warden replied to Joseph's sister, Mrs. Melvin Kaatz, in October 1939: "… In reply, kindly be advised that his was a sudden death and without pain…. He did have a watch and a few personal effects but only 42 cents on deposit and as his son, Russell Flitcraft, was at the institution this morning, those effects were given to him." The family didn't have the thirty-five dollars plus transportation costs to claim Joseph's body, so the prison sent his body to the State Medical School in Bloomington.

By 1940 Iris and Russell lived in Boone County in a house they rented for seven dollars a month. Russell enlisted in the army in February 1943. A year later, Russell and Iris lived in Bangor, Maine. Russell left the army in January 1946.

Iris suffered numerous miscarriages and didn't believe she would be able to carry a child to term. She and Russell, in 1948, learned about a single mother who was unable to care for her three children. When they arrived at the home, they saw a dirty two-year-old girl chewing on a piece of rotten potato. Russell took the three siblings to a restaurant to get something to eat. Iris stayed behind and reached an agreement with the mother to adopt the two-year-old child. Iris promised the child would never go hungry, and they would send her to college. She spent the next twelve months worrying the mother would change her mind and come back to claim Judith. But she never did.

Iris and Russell's two-day-old son, James, died in May 1949. Russell died in November 1984. Iris said she didn't want to live to be ninety years old, and she died the day after her ninetieth birthday in March 2008 in Boone County. Iris' granddaughter, Lisa Haughton, recalled that Iris loved playing Euchre and was a "wonderful cook." Iris enjoyed politics and in a different day and age might have run for office. Iris and Russell also provided a foster home for several children. Lisa shared how "Iris was smitten with her grandchildren and great grandchildren and they brought her an abundance of joy". Russell and Iris had two children: James and Judith Adams.

CHAPTER 10: PAULINE
AND ALBEN FOOTE

Rose first mentioned Pauline on the first day of 1935 when she wrote: "The roads are very slick. Alberta, Pauline and Lois with some of the boys went to Sunday School Class Meeting." Alben received his first and only mention nine months later when Rose noted "Alben Foote returned."

Jay Waldo Foote and Elizabeth "Bessie" Emery married in Chicago in February 1917. John E. Terria shared how he believed Bessie's family encouraged her to marry Jay, a man from a wealthy family, but one she didn't love. Their first child, Edward, was born two days before Christmas in 1917. Pauline Florence was born ten days before Christmas in 1918.

By early 1920, Edward and Pauline lived in a rented house in LaSalle County, Illinois with their parents, who farmed. Blue-eyed Alben James was born on the twentieth of April 1920 in LaSalle County, Illinois. Jay and Bessie also had Helen, born in April 1924 in Ohio, and Byron, born in January 1926 in Ohio.

The White County Juvenile Court sent Pauline, Alben, and their older eleven-year-old brother Edward to the Welfare Home in August 1929. Presumably Bessie could not care for all five children. Jay and Bessie likely divorced about this time. Authorities described both

Alben and Pauline as "placeable." They also described Alben as "good natured." In September 1930, authorities sent Edward to live with James M. Smith near Warsaw. A state report from December 1931 on Edward noted: "… Edward died 10-1-31, with acute indigestion…. The county was notified, and they took care of a part of the funeral expenses. The Mother, Bessie Aldena Emery Foote, was also notified but did not come." A year earlier Bessie lived with her parents and two children, five-year-old Helen and four-year-old Bryon, on Linden Street in Monon.

Bessie, John E. and John Terria
(John E. Terria)

Bessie married a Yugoslavian shoe repairman, John Terria, after her divorce from Jay. Some time around 1950, Bessie filed for divorce from John. Fifty-four-year-old Bessie Terria died at the Logansport State Hospital in February 1952. Her death certificate noted she suffered from psychosis. John died six months later.

On the last day of May 1933, Alben lived with Mrs. Mary Reinholt at rural Winamac. A state report on Alben nine months later noted: "He helps in fact he practically does all of the caring for some 14 or 15 hogs, 2 cows and a horse or two. Boy states he does not have an opportunity to take a bath. Boy says with the exception of washing his neck and ears and feet he has not had a bath since last summer when he could go to the creek." The report described the foster mother as "almost helpless, is very heavy. Can scarcely walk. Is almost deaf. She seems to very anxious for boy to be in her home, but her object is no doubt entirely a selfish one."

The state agent continued: "This home is very unsatisfactory and other plans should be made for this boy.... The boy should be in a home where there is an interested, firm, sympathetic foster father who will teach him the things a boy of his age should know regarding life and also teach him to work.... Other than food, clothing and a bed there is nothing in the Reinholt home."

In May 1935 a state report on Alben noted: "Boy has two or three cavities in his teeth. Foster Mother stated she did not know about these. Boy told Visitor that he had not told her. Visitor asked her if she could have these cared for. She would make no promises. Foster Mother is one of those old fashioned, stingy German type who is extremely hard to convince how necessary it is for matters of this kind to be given attention. Boy complained about the food. He states it is the same thing over practically every day. He would like to have milk to drink.... After she would not give him milk, he asked her to make him some cocoa occasionally. She will not do this. Visitor asked Foster Mother if boy could have a quart of whole milk a day and she told Visitor that she has to have all her whole milk to help her meet her grocery bill and other expenses. Visitor asked her then if she would let boy have a glass of whole milk every day. She would not promise this. She remarked 'I suppose he has been complaining about his food'.... She stated that she prepares the food and puts it on the table, and he can eat what she puts on the table…. There is no doubt an abundance of wholesome food in his home that could be very appetizingly prepared if the Foster Mother would do it herself or permit anybody else to do so. The family was called to the noon meal before Visitor left. There was meat and potatoes and beans and apple sauce, different kinds of jellies. Boy had stated that it was the same thing every day and that if anything spoils before the small family can eat it, it is cooked over and doctored up and the dish is often set between him and Maggie Hardinger, the old lady who stays with Mrs. Reinholt."

On the first day of September 1935, the Superintendent returned Alben to the Welfare Home. Records noted "…. in many ways it was unfit for a boy to be with such an aged lady as Mrs. Reinholt, who besides being aged is crippled and extremely hard of hearing."

In November, Pauline and Alben's brother, Byron, attracted national attention. A St. Louis newspaper reported: "Boy, 9, Found Living in Open Like Primitive Man." Byron and his stepfather, John Terria didn't get along very well and nine-year-old Byron lived in a homemade hut in a cornfield. After living with neighbors for a few months, authorities sent Byron to the Mexico Welfare Home, in July 1936, after "he had not been receiving proper care."

In 1934, a sixteen-year-old Pauline asked for a "mouth harp or green shirt and blouse, size 36" for Christmas. On the eighteenth of January, Rose cleaned and spent part of the afternoon working over Pauline's "lavender dress." On the second day of February, Pauline became sick. Rose wrote "We did our cleaning this morning and I put Pauline to bed, doctoring her good later. Mrs. Rarick put a mustard plaster on her chest and back." On the fourth day of May, Rose made Pauline an orange and brown checked dress.

On the first of July, Rose noted: "Some of the girls washed while we got supper and at 8 o'clock we are through and have did a big day's work. Pauline ironed a lot of shirts & towels, etc. So, we will try to have some play tomorrow." Five days later, Rose helped Pauline mop the dorm room. Pauline may not have had strong sewing skills, since on the eighteenth of July Rose wrote: "I made Pauline's dress today that she tried to make in domestic class & failed." A week later, Rose made Pauline a green silk blouse. Days later Rose noted: "New shoes for Marjorie, Iris, Alberta and Pauline."

Pauline went to live with Mr. and Mrs. Roland Fain at 1118 S. Calumet Street in Kokomo in August 1936. The Fains returned Pauline in February 1937 due to "Mr. Fain's employment being uncertain." In April 1937, they placed Pauline with Mr. and Mrs. Frank Phelps.

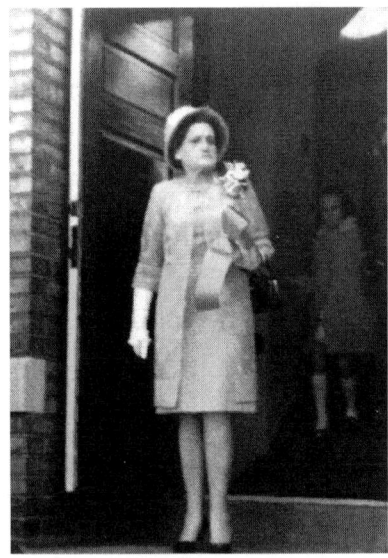

Pauline Foote McClain
(John E. Terria)

Pauline married Cecil McClain at Kokomo in May 1939. Cecil died in September 1966. Pauline died in late January 1992 at Huntington. In an undated newspaper article in Marion's Chronicle Tribune, Pauline said "If God had wanted people to ride, he would have given us wheels instead of feet." Duane Jones interviewed Pauline and wrote "She doesn't own a car, never has. She's never driven one, doesn't plan to learn… figures she walks five or 10 miles a day… walks to church once or twice a week and never misses a benefit fish fry or chicken dinner. She attends band concerts, political rallies, parades, 4-H fairs, groundbreaking ceremonies, anniversaries, and horseshoe tournaments."

On the first of June 1937, authorities placed Alben and Byron with Mr. and Mrs. Ross Sills at Winchester Road in Fort Wayne. Thirteen-year-old Byron died in late August 1939 after his third bout with pneumonia.

Alben enlisted in the United States Army in September 1939. In late April 1948, Alben either lived or worked at the Grand-Pine Hotel at 206 North Grand Boulevard in St. Louis.

Thirty-year-old Alben married Ruth L. McFall in St. Louis in September 1950. He showed it was his first marriage while Ruth, born in June 1914, was a widow. Alben died in December 1968 and was buried in Huntington County. Alben was married twice and had no children.

Alben and Ruth Foote
(John E. Terria)

CHAPTER 11: MARTHA JOAN GALBREATH

Rose first mentioned Martha Joan on the twenty-eighth of March when she "remodeled some of Anna Lou's dresses for Joan."

Martha Joan was born on the thirtieth of July 1920 to Roy Lee Galbreath and Lena Etha Rider at Pierceton. Her older sister, Myrtle Alice, arrived in October 1916. Lena died in 1924 from chronic interstitial nephritis.

In 1928 a school health record described Martha's home conditions as "poor" and showed that eight children were in the home with no mother. Roy earned seven hundred dollars a year, and the health record described him as having a "poor" interest in both girls and their schooling. The girls weighed less than normal for their age. Myrtle suffered "frontal headaches" possibly related to a vision problem.

Myrtle's father, Roy signed her seventh-grade report card for Pierceton High School in 1929/1930. She missed nineteen days of school and her grades were "fair, below" in every subject. An Elizabeth Galbreath signed Martha's report card for 1929/1930 school year. The report showed she missed fifteen days of school and had a B or C average in all subjects.

Nine-year-old Martha and her sister, blue-eyed Myrtle, came to the home on the twenty-third of April 1930 because of a court order.

Fifteen-year-old Myrtle Alice died at Pierceton from meningitis in May 1932. The Welfare Home described her as "a No.1 girl." Rose only mentioned Martha twice. On the twenty-ninth of March, Rose noted "After dinner I finished mending hose, then remade a dress for Joan."

In 1940 nineteen-year-old Martha Joan lived with Donald and Mary Holbrook in Kosciusko County and kept house for them. Donald farmed and Mary worked at the post office. Martha had worked for Donald and Mary for the past twenty weeks. The same year her father, Roy, a widow, farmed in Koscuisko County and lived with his son, Moody.

Martha married Bud Walls in March 1941. Bud died in May 1986. Martha retired from Pierceton Foods and attended the Warsaw Pleasant Grove United Methodist Church. Eighty-eight-year-old Martha Joan Walls died in July 2009 at Winnona Lake. Cause of death was a "failure to thrive" and "vascular dementia." Martha and Bud had one son, Wendell.

CHAPTER 12:
ANNABELLE GLASSBURN

Annabelle received her first mention from Rose on the fifth of January 1935 when she noted: "Annabelle, June, Phyllis and Myrtle have been in bed today but are up for supper."

Annabelle Glassburn was born on the tenth of June 1923 to Benjamin Glassburn and Miranda Sopher Austin. Benjamin married Miranda in May 1919 at Peru. This was the second marriage for both.

Sixteen-year-old Florence Marie Weaver of Peru kidnapped three-month-old Annabelle in 1923. Florence said she "kidnapped the child to even up an old score resulting from a family feud." A Fort Wayne newspaper described the incident. "The Weaver girl is known to have a mania for children. She took the baby when the members of the Glassburn family were in the rear of the house and the baby was asleep in its crib in one of the front rooms. The Weaver girl quietly entered the front door, which was not locked, wrapped the baby in a little blanket, making it look like a bundle, and went out the same way she had entered. The girl is believed to be subnormal mentally." Authorities located Florence and Annabelle in Hammond. They were on their way to Chicago.

Police also arrested Florence's mother after the kidnapping. She denied being involved but had been with Florence when she purchased a train ticket to Chicago. Florence's father died in a Michigan State Prison while serving a life sentence for molesting her. Florence received a three-month sentence and left prison in November 1923. She married Bryan Zeck in July 1924 at Logansport and died in July 1950 at Logansport.

In September 1918, a forty-year-old Benjamin worked as a teamster at the Canal Elevator at Peru and lived at 363 Washington Street in Peru. Two years later, a forty-two-year-old Benjamin lived in a rented house at 327 East Second Street with his twenty-four-year-old wife, Miranda and three children.

By 1920, fifty-three-year-old Miranda lived at 254 Third Street in Peru with her father, four children, and a daughter-in-law. Glenna Hepworth said "Miranda and Benjamin divorced due to abuse. She sought refuge for a time with two aunts in Peru." Thirty-one-year-old Miranda died in January 1927 from cancer in Peru.

On the twenty-ninth of January 1930, Annabelle and Cassie May came to the Welfare Home. Annabelle was placed on the sixth of May 1934 with Mr. and Mrs. Harry C. Miller at 802 N. Seventh Street in Goshen. The Millers returned her on the eighth of May 1934 due to the fact that "she would not be contented."

In 1934, eleven-year-old Annabelle asked for a "comb set or beads" for Christmas. On the tenth of January 1935, Rose noted that "Priscilla & Annabelle have gone to bed this afternoon- fever & headache." The next day Rose said: "I did the morning cleaning and took care of the sick girls Priscilla, Annabelle, Myrtle, and Olivine. I am almost sick with a cold."

Three days later, Rose said "Myrtle & Annabelle are feeling better this evening." On the fifteenth of January, Rose noted: "Seems we can't get straightened up from sickness. Annabelle & Myrtle do not feel well yet."

On the thirtieth of March, Rose noted: "June & Annabelle went to class today." On the fourth of June, Rose "Worked at a made over dress for Annabelle." Rose finished the dress the next day. On the last day of July, Rose helped Pauline and Annabelle "take care of the dining room yet today." On the twenty-ninth of October, Rose wrote: "Went to church. Iris & Annabelle & Thelma joined." On the sixteenth of November, Rose noted that Annabelle went to the hospital to visit her father. Benjamin died in March 1943 at Peru.

Three days after Christmas 1938, Annabelle went to the Charles Wasiner home near Cassville. She came back to the Welfare Home and then lived with Mr. and Mrs. Oscar Caplinger at 2150 N. Rural Street, Indianapolis. She returned to the Welfare Home from the Caplinger home on the twenty-second of March 1941. On the thirtieth of April, they placed Annabelle with Dr. John P. Landgrave of Peru. Annabelle went back to the Welfare Home on the twenty-eighth of July 1941 until "woman is again in the work home." Mrs. Landgrave soon returned home, and Annabelle left the Welfare Home on the seventh of August 1941 to return to Dr. Landgraves. Five days later, Mrs. Bauer returned Annabelle to the home. "Annabelle had been dissatisfied and left Landgraves, without Mrs. Bauer's permission, under the influence of relatives."

Annabelle periodically shows up in the Welfare Home records through October 1941. She received a discharge on the twelfth of October. In May 1943, Annabelle used the last name of Tyler. Twenty-two-year-old Annabelle Tyler married Emerson L. Rains in March 1945. A divorced Annabelle Nulph married Raymond Zimmerman in August 1950 in Fulton County. During the early seventies, Annabelle and Raymond lived at 31 North Cardinal Avenue in Stockton, California. Annabelle died in August 2002 in Stockton, California. Raymond Zimmerman died in January 2002 at Lodi, California.

On the thirteenth of August 1931, they placed Cassie with Mrs. Gustave Becker at Peru. Miranda died on the twenty-third day of May 1932 at sixty-five from diabetes. A state report in July 1934 on Cassie noted ".... The father, Benjamin Franklin Glassburn, lives in Peru. Occasionally visits. Is not working much but in past year has made gifts to the girl. A cousin of whom the girl was very fond and who visited, her, Leona Glassburn, died.... The contact with the father does not interfere."

Cassie married Frederick Eugene Orpurt in November 1939. Glenna Hepworth shared the following about Cassie: "I met my brother Errol in the late 1990's.... His mother Cassie May was by far a victim of circumstances. Her parents either separated, divorced, or Miranda passed away, but given the history... I would say she probably ran away from her husband who was abusive.... Cassie and her sister were placed in what was then the Mexico Old Folks Home and Orphanage.... Cassie was nine when she was placed in there. After spending years there, Fred Orpurt must have negotiated to have Cassie released in order to marry. She was 16. He did NOT take her sister out though. Errol told me that this was something she had a difficult time dealing with. Fred then left Cassie shortly after she gave birth to my brother." Cassie died in January 1976.

CHAPTER 13: LUTHER, THURMAN, AND ERMALINE GLASSBURN

Rose first mentioned brown eyed Ermaline on the eighth of January 1935. "… This morning Ermaline and I mopped after breakfast." On the thirtieth of June, Rose wrote that "Luther Glassburn went with his brother for the day." In late August Rose wrote: "Thurman Glassburn came back."

A twenty-nine-year-old Gilbert Glassburn married seventeen-year-old Ina Roubenault in November 1910 at Peru. Ina was born in 1893 in Miami County. In September 1918, Gilbert worked as a "farm laborer" for a Montgomery in Barnes County, North Dakota. Two years later, thirty-eight-year-old Gilbert Glassburn, a laborer for the railroad, lived at 128 Maple Street in Peru in a rented home with his twenty-six-year-old wife and four children.

Geraldine, LaVerta, Virgil, Luther, Thurman, and Ermaline Glassburn came to the Welfare Home on the twenty-fourth of July or August 1925 from Miami County. But Thurman recalled the tenth of August 1924 as the date because of their parents separating. Geraldine was born in 1913. LaVerta in 1914. Virgil in 1916. Luther 1919. Thurman 1920, and Ermaline in 1921.

Ina's obituary noted that "She was first married to Gilbert Glassburn… in 1910. Following his death, she was married to Claude Zimmerman in 1926." But the 1930 census showed that a divorced Gilbert lived at 318 West Canal Street in Peru with his mother, Alice, a brother and a nephew, and worked at odd jobs. A divorced fifty-two-year-old Gilbert died in November 1933; four days short of his birthday. Thirty-six-year-old Iva Zimmerman lived in Miami County in 1930 with her twenty-five-year-old husband and twins: Robert and Sammy Zimmerman. Claude died in 1932. Ina Belle Zimmerman died in 1956.

For Christmas 1927 seven-year-old Thurman asked for a tool chest. Eight-year-old Luther wanted an erector set, while fourteen-year-old Geraldine asked for a coat and hat. LaVerta, then thirteen years old, asked for a sweater and red cap, and five-year-old Ermaline wanted a go-cart.

Rose never mentioned the other Glassburn siblings in her journals. Welfare officials placed LaVerta with a Mr. Marks at Huntington in December 1929. In 1930, LaVerta worked as a "servant" at 1117 Jefferson in Huntington for the August and Ione Wasmuth family.

A state report in April 1930 on LaVerta shared: "county authorities follow being slow at work and so backward." In December 1930, a state report noted "is interested in taking a business course or nurses training after she has finished her high school course. Attends Sunday School. LaVerta's conduct is above complaint."

LaVerta married F. Clyde Boner in July 1934. In 1940, she lived with her husband, a four-year-old daughter, and her nineteen-year-old brother, Thurman. A widowed seventy-nine-year-old LaVerta died at her daughter's home at 1324 Engle Street in Peru in July 1994.

Geraldine was born on the seventh of April 1913. In 1930, seventeen-year-old Geraldine, a maid, lived at 1145 Jefferson Street in Huntington with the Lewis and Irma Marx family. A state report in May 1930 on Geraldine noted: "Conduct is fair. Girl is stubborn. Foster Mother told Visitor that there are times when she will ask girl to do work a certain way and the girl will just stop and look at her and say nothing…. Visitor talked with girl concerning her work and attitude. Girl cried and told Visitor that she will try to do better." A December state report on Geraldine shared: "Has trouble with her legs swelling but the Foster Mother states that it is something probably hereditary…. Conduct is above complaint with the exception that there has been a few times which Geraldine has pouted but the Foster Mother stated she has talked to Geraldine a great deal about this and she is doing so much better in her conduct."

Geraldine married William Floyd Weaver. In 1946 and 1949, Geraldine and Floyd lived at 245 Jackson Street in Huntington. Forty-year-old Geraldine Izora Weaver died in September 1953 at Columbia City.

Virgil Niel or Nile Glassburn was born in April 1916 at Peru. His birth certificate showed Niel, and the Social Security Index showed Nile. They placed Virgil with A.F. Wasmuth at Huntington on the fourteenth of January 1930. Months later, a thirteen-year-old Virgil lived with Leroy and Nora Wildman and worked as their "helper." By May 1930 a state report on Virgil noted: "will be given piano lessons this summer. Attends Sunday school. Does light work and chores about the home."

A state report on Virgil in February 1931 noted: "…. Foster Father stated boy has not failed him yet." They returned Virgil in late March 1931. Five months later, in August 1931, they sent him to White's Institute at Fort Wayne. Virgil married June Olinger in October 1941. She died in 1972. Virgil lived at Huntington in 1956. He died in March 1992 in Sebring, Florida. Virgil was a Huntington Local 103 operating engineer.

Luther Laven Glassburn was born on the third of April 1919 at Peru. They placed him with LaRoy Willman at Denver in February 1930. A late April 1930 census showed that Luther was back at the home. The home described Luther as "friendly," "truthful," and not "quick to anger." In 1934, a fifteen-year-old Luther asked for a "mechanical toy or Chemcraft or book of 200 tricks" for Christmas.

He married Garnett Louise Newman. In 1994, Luther lived at Amboy. He died two days after Christmas in 2002. Luther and Garnett had at least two children: Thomas L. Glassburn and Joan Figg.

Blue-eyed Thurman Thurl Glassburn was born at Peru on the fourteenth of September 1920. In 1930 he lived with his siblings at the Welfare Home in Mexico.

Thurman recalled his time at the home: "The county paid 24 cents daily for each person kept there during those Depression years. Glassburn was four when he went to the orphanage, which became his home for about 13 years. 'Most of the time it was a happy place for us,' he said. In the summer, the children helped with the truck patch where the orphanage raised its own vegetables, planting, weeding, harvesting… the work was done by two horses … the children brushed their teeth with salt… at Christmas time, toys were collected at J.C. Penny, Peru, for the children in the orphanage. 'I got a sled one time,' Glassburn remembered. 'It really meant a lot to me, because I had never had anything'…. At church there were 9 or 10 pews filled with children on each side. Glassburn remembers that the first superintendent of the home, whose name was Fisher, used to come and visit. 'Everybody liked him," he said. "The kids kind of worshipped him. They really liked him. He was so nice to everyone.' Glassburn was too small and wasn't allowed to go swimming during the drownings…. Relatives were allowed to come and visit the children every weekend. "I had a grandfather who came. I thought a lot of him, because he was the only one who came and visited. He was the only close relative I had.' Among the mentors from his school years is an invoice dated April 19, 1937 that showed the Vandeweghe Trading Corp., N.Y., had purchased 47 rabbit skins for a total of $4.40. The children helped raise the rabbits, which were used for food. The orphanage officials let them sell the skins.... Glassburn was placed several times in homes that proved unsatisfactory, and he was brought back to the orphanage. Eventually, however, he found a home with I.H. Ulrich in Huntington County. Ulrich was township accessor of Lancaster Township... his oldest sister got married a little later (after he graduated high school). She got him a job in the factory where her husband was foreman, and Glassburn went out on his own."

Thurman went on to say "On several occasions I was placed in private homes, beginning in 1933. I left for the last time in 1937 to live with my mother in Huntington County. That was my first year of high school. While in the Home I learned to know some of the trustees quite well and they had an influence in my life. There was Walter Balsbaugh, also a minister, who baptized me. I recall standing nearby, eavesdropping, when Marion Miller was explaining to some other men how one of the old folks had turned all of his property over to the Home for his keep, only to learn later that it was all mortgaged for more than it was worth. We all loved Marion Miller."

In June 1934, they placed Thurman with Mr. and Mrs. Perry Shively at Bunker Hill. By the end of August 1935, he was back at the home. "The boy was overworked. Also, the attitude of the foster parents too critical and nagging." Thurman recalled receiving a sled for Christmas while at the home. "I'll always remember the special Christmas season when I had hoped to get a sled and sure enough someone had made my wish come true."

A state report on Thurman in July 1934 from Phebe Jeffers noted: "Visitor advised boy to get acquainted with some boys, get into Sunday School and get acquainted as it will help him when he starts to school in fall…. Foster Mother, in Visitor's opinion, is only interested in the boy for the work he can do…. Boy seems like a very good type who needs an opportunity."

A state report in June 1935 noted: "Thurman is a fairly bright boy…. Foster parents stated they do not have any complaint…. but he is very slow and forgetful…. The boy is rather retiring in disposition and does not care to mix very much in society." On the eighteenth of November 1935, Rose wrote "Thurman & Russell have mumps." In May 1937 they placed him with his mother at Denver.

By 1940, a nineteen-year-old Thurman lived with his sister, LaVerta Boner, and her husband in Huntington. In July 1945, "T-Sgt. Thurman T. Glassburn, 245 Jackson St., Huntington" arrived in Charleston, South Carolina, for a furlough. He was a member of the 15th Army Air Force in Italy. Twenty-six-year-old Thurman married Viola M. Davenriner in July 1946 in Indiana. In 1954 and 1957, Thurman and Viola lived at 409 Gardendale Avenue, Huntington, and he worked as a "carrier." Thurman married Dorothy Helen Barrett in January 1983 at Wabash.

Ermaline Levina Glassburn was born on the twelfth of December 1921 in Miami County. Ermaline lived at the home in 1930. A state report from April 1932 from Phebe Jeffers on Ermaline noted "Teacher stated that girl is slow, probably doing all that she is capable of doing. Does not attend Sunday school and church as there is no way for her to go to the nearest church in Amboy…. Foster Mother may put more work on the girl than she is old enough to do."

A state report in May 1933 on Ermaline noted: "Visitor feels child should have a thorough physical examination. Foster Mother states ears bad when child came to her home. Girl also has bad teeth. Girl has an enlarged gland in neck and one under jaw…. These Foster Parents are old and in very poor health and likely will not exert themselves very much toward getting girl to a physician…. Foster Mother states it seems very difficult for girl to learn and feels she has always been promoted because it seemed more advisable for her to go along with children of her own age rather than have her repeating school grade."

The state report went on to say: "When Visitor first went to this home Foster Mother made a great many complaints about the child, that she is stubborn, that she a great many times will not answer her when called, and stated that when she got the child she wanted a larger one who could be more help to her and wondered if there is any older girl she could secure and also went on to state that the Foster Father never did like the girl and it makes him out of patience when girl looks at him."

Maud Williams the state agent described the foster parents as "old, sick and crabby. No doubt their sole interest in child is the help she can render them." On the twenty-sixth of May 1931, they placed Ermaline with W.S. Johnson at Amboy. On the twelfth of June 1933, a state visit found the home "unsatisfactory." A thirteen-year-old Ermaline asked for a "manicure set" for Christmas in 1934.

On the twelfth of January 1935, Rose shared: "Ermaline and I cleaned the dorm and I mopped the other 2 rooms too. Then I went to bed. Have been in bed all afternoon. I must be having flu." On the eleventh of February, Rose started sewing a blouse for Ermaline. She finished the blouse the next day. Rose, on the fourth of March, noted: "I mended clothes for several girls and made a dress for Ermaline." On the eighth of April, Rose wrote: "Marjorie & Ermaline are sick in bed." Rose, on the fifth of May, noted "Ermaline and Marjorie did not go to church. Rose, in late June, wrote: "Ermaline went to Mr. Martz of Huntington today where Geraldine used to be." On the first day of November Rose noted: "The Superintendent and Matron went to Huntington. Brought Ermaline back." They placed Ermaline and brown-eyed Luther on the fourth of May 1937 with their mother, Iva Zimmerman, at Denver.

Seventeen-year-old Ermaline married Claude L. Coldren in December 1938. An eighteen-year-old Ermaline lived with her husband and son in Erie Township, Miami County, in 1940. In September 1942, Ermaline filed for divorce from Claude. "Charging her husband... with cruelty, failure to provide and association with other women.... She seeks a support allowance of $10 a week, custody of two children, and a restraining order to enjoin the defendant from "striking, wounding, beating, or in any way assaulting or molesting this plaintiff. She says that he has beaten her and their two children, aged two and three, respectively."

Twenty-four-year-old Ermaline married Earl E. Ellet in July 1945. A divorced seventy-two-year-old Ermaline died in May 1994 at Huntington.

CHAPTER 14: THELMA MAE AND JAMES GLASSBURN

Rose first mentioned Thelma on the fifth day of February 1935. "I have dampened clothes and then I sewed at Thelma's blue print dress until it was time to carry dinner over to first floor. This afternoon I did my ironing, finished Thelma's and my dress that Mother gave me, and before supper started Marjorie's dress. Have it all done by 9 o'clock. It snowed quite a lot today." On the last day of June 1935 Rose noted: "James Glassburn called a while. It is so warm."

Thelma, five-years old, and her siblings, nine-year-old James and seven-year-old Leona Ellen, arrived at the Welfare Home on the twenty-second of October 1928 from Huntington County. Thelma Glassburn was born on the third day of January 1923 in Miami County to Noah Glassburn and Mary Leona Sopher. She was the youngest of three children.

In June 1917, a single Noah gave his occupation as a "Checker" at the C & O Freight Office. He showed he supported a "mother & child." Thirty-one-year-old Noah married sixteen-year-old Mary Sopher in April 1918. Mary Leona was born in February 1903 and died in May 1970. In 1920, Noah, Mary, and James lived at 256 West Second Street in Peru, where he worked as a "checker" in the "Steam RR."

By 1930 a divorced Noah lived at 318 West Canal Street in Peru with his mother, Alice, where he worked "odd jobs" at a box factory. Also, in the home were Noah's forty-eight-year-old divorced brother, Gilbert, and fourteen-year-old Verlin G. Haines, a grandson of Alice Glassburn. A 1930 Welfare Home report showed Noah to be an "invalid." Forty-three-year-old Noah died in July 1930. Mary lived with her parents in a rented home on West Seventh Street in Peru in 1930. Also, in the home was Mary's four-year-old daughter, Helen Glassburn.

Mary divorced Chester A. Manus, in March 1935 and went back to using the Glassburn name. She married John Shilling at Wabash the same month. A widowed Mary died in Peru in May 1970 at sixty-seven years of age.

In 1930, seven-year-old Thelma lived at the Welfare Home with her two siblings. Thelma's sister, a thirteen-year-old Leona Ellen, died on the eighteenth of May 1934 at the home from diabetes. The same year, a fifteen-year-old James asked for an "ocarina or harmonica and holder, key G" for Christmas. Eleven-year-old Thelma asked for a "toy baking set or electric stove."

Rose wrote on the fourth of April some of the children tested positive for Tuberculosis. "Dr. & nurse has been here to see children. Found Lewis positive. Lois also & Thelma G., & Myrtle. Rose may have referred to Thelma Glassburn rather than Thelma Gorney. On the twenty-sixth of June, Rose noted: "Mr. & Mrs. Rarick took Thelma near Logansport, but the place was not satisfactory-Brot her back." On the twenty-ninth of October, Rose wrote "Went to church. Iris & Annabelle & Thelma joined." It is possible that Rose was referring to Thelma Gorney rather than Glassburn.

In mid-November, on a Sunday Rose wrote: "Thelma Glassburn's mother brought her a Victrola." In 1935, Thelma said she lived on a farm in Nappanee, Kosciusko County. In September 1936, Thelma spent a "trial period" with Mr. and Mrs. Arvella McClain of Nappanee. She was back to the home at the end of August 1938. The next month they placed her with the Charles Waisner family near Cassville. Seventeen-year-old Thelma lived in Howard County in 1940. Also, in the home were Charles and Hester Waisner and Shirley and Mary Steffa.

Twenty-three-year-old Thelma married Seth Huddleston in October 1946 in Indiana. Seth died in March 1985 in Cass County. Ten years later in May 1995, Thelma married Orville Bailey. Orville had also lived at the Welfare Home. He died in December 2003.

Thelma died on the eighteenth of October 2012 in Roanoke, Virginia. She worked as a registered nurse at the Logansport State Hospital. She graduated from high school in Howard County in 1940 and nursing school in 1946. Thelma was a member of the Logansport Church of the Brethren and served as church treasurer. Thelma and Seth had one son: David Huddleston.

James Allen Glassburn was born on the fifth of February 1919. In 1920 he lived on West Second Street in Peru with his parents. On the seventh of September 1931, authorities placed James with Leon Sheetz of Akron. By the fourth of October 1931 the Sheetz returned him due to his being 'unruly." Mrs. M. Norris had recommended against placing a child in their home again because "need a farm hand instead of child."

James went on a vacation in late June 1935 and came back a month later, and they noted that "Mother caused trouble." In October 1935 they enrolled him at C.C.C. Camp at Kokomo for six months. James, in 1940, lived with his mother and stepfather, John Shilling at Pipe Creek in Miami County. His stepfather was four years older than James. James worked as a laborer for six hundred dollars a year.

He married Bernice Mettler in March 1941. James enlisted in the army in November 1944. He showed he had two years of high school and worked for a semi-skilled machine shop operation. He served for two years and received a discharge in November 1946. In 1947, James, a lathe operator, and Bernice lived in Peru. Seventy-one-year-old James, a former sheet metal worker, died in October 1990 in Marion.

Thelma, David and Seth Huddleston
(Rose Scholl Family)

CHAPTER 15: THELMA AND BETTY GORNEY

By early April 1935, Thelma lived at the Welfare Home in Mexico. She may have been there at least two months earlier, as Rose noted she spent part of the day sewing on a blue dress for a girl named Thelma. On the fourth of November 1935, Rose noted "Betty Gorney has been adopted by the Williams family of Michigan City and left today."

Sixteen-year-old Ida Poyser gave birth to Thelma on the twentieth of June 1919 in Peru. Thelma's death certificate listed her father as Paul Deitter. Paul may have been Paul Deeter, who was born in 1901 and died in 1977 in Miami County. He married Ruetta "Pearl" Tibbets in 1926.

Seventeen-year-old Ida and Thelma lived with Ida's parents in Jefferson Township, Miami County, in 1920. Four years later, twenty-two-year-old Ida Ann married a blue-eyed thirty-two-year-old Louis Joseph Gorney at Peru in February.

Betty Jean Gorney entered the world on the sixth of March 1926 in Peru. By April 1930, Louis and Ida had two children, five-year-old Mary Louise and four-year-old Betty Jean. But twenty-seven-year-old Ida still lived with her parents, and Louis' whereabouts are unknown. Also, in the home on East Eighth Street in Peru was a ten-year-old

Thelma. Betty and her sister Mary Louise and perhaps Thelma came to the Welfare Home on the twelfth of January 1932. On the fourth of May 1932, they placed Betty with Mr. and Mrs. Allen Williams of East Chicago. On the fifth of September 1933 the Williams' returned Betty and noted they were "unable financially to keep her." Perhaps they missed her and six days later Betty was back in their home.

John Potocki's mother, Betty Jean, shared with him that Ida, a tiny woman, had a sixth sense about things. Ida worked as a waitress and could not support the two girls, but she came to the home and visited with them regularly.

Betty had her own bed, at the Williams, in the same room as her eleven-year-old foster brother, Robert Allen Williams and eighteen-year-old Dorothy Underwood. Thirty-seven-year-old Allen Williams worked as a fireman for the Northern Indiana Public Service Company. Both he and his wife were said to have "average health."

Three months later, their father, Louis, was arrested on charges of petty larceny related to fraudulent checks to a Cari Dillman of Twelve Mile.

A state report for Betty in September noted: "Agent called on Mrs. Allen Williams..... who stated that they had returned Betty Jean.... Foster Mother said they were all cut up by the fact that they had to take Betty Jean back, but their finances would not permit them to keep her. Stated when they are financially better off they would like to have girl back."

Eight months later, Ida Gorney went to see a Miami County Judge and prompted him to write to the home: "Mrs. Ida Gorney of 256 East 8th St., Peru, is now in my office, and she is desirous of having her girl, Thelma Gorney, now an inmate at your home, fourteen years of age, to visit her for two weeks. If this meets your approval, I have no objections."

Thelma, on a cloudy and damp early April day, helped Rose hang clothes in the dryers. Two weeks later Rose made a dress for Thelma by using one of Myrtle's brown shirts and reworking a dress from Thelma's mother.

In early May, Thelma and Lois went to an evening show. Nine days later, Rose remade a dress for a Thelma and worked on one for Louise. After completing their work in mid-May, the girls went fishing after dinner. Rose noted "Got no fish but a lot of greens. And Lois & Thelma Gorney got a few mushrooms. We had a "green" feed since supper." A month later in June Rose made a dress for Thelma.

Late in August Rose cut out a striped dress for Thelma. In September, Ida filed for divorce in Miami County alleging "cruel and inhuman treatment" and asked for custody of Mary and Betty.

A divorced seventy-two-year-old Louis, a World War I veteran and sheet metal worker, died in May 1965 in Parke County. He had contracted tuberculous while working at the Rockville Sanatorium. John Potocki remembered going there and waving to Louis through the fence.

On Visiting Day Rose noted that Thelma's mother was one of two parents who came to visit their children. Three days later, Rose cut out dresses for Thelma and Ada. They placed Thelma with her aunt, Mrs. William Sutton of Peru on the twenty-ninth of August 1936. On the fifth of January 1938, Thelma was "Returned home from Williams in Michigan City where Thelma's sister is adopted." On the twenty-third of February, Thelma went to Indianapolis to be fitted for corrective shoes and glasses at the Akron Surgical House. In July 1938, they placed Thelma with the Waisners nears Cassville. They returned her three days before Christmas because of medical issues.

On the seventh of March 1939, Thelma had two teeth filled and in late May she had a tooth filled and another removed. On the thirtieth of April, Thelma moved in with her mother at Peru.

Twenty-year-old Thelma Marie Gorney married thirty-two-year-old Edward James Rider in late September 1939 in Indiana. By January 1941, Thelma used the last name of Poyser. Twenty-seven-year old Thelma M. Poyser married forty-four-year-old Floyd Rominger on the eleventh of March 1946 at Peru. Floyd died in 1970.

In 1952 Thelma M. Rominger lived at Madison, Wisconsin where she worked as an aid. By January 1954, Thelma and Floyd lived at 222 East Eighth Street in Peru. Thelma and Betty's mother, Ida, died in 1968. She worked at the Peru Laundry.

Thelma married Lawrence "Larry" Harbert in Logansport on April Fool's day 1972. In 1992 Thelma Marie Rominger lived in Bristol Tennessee and in Richmond, Virginia. Thelma had a leg amputated later in life. Eighty-three-year-old Thelma M. Deitter Harbert died on Christmas Day 2002 at Logansport.

A report for Betty in January 1935 showed that: "Her general health is good…. she has very bad tonsils…. Betty does not have the life about her that she should have. That she is rather delicate…. She is not hard to control. Attends religious services regularly."

On the fifth of July, nine-year-old Betty was returned to the Welfare Home from the Williams at 401 East Michigan Street in Michigan City. The home noted "Brought back by Mrs. Allen Williams, who had had Betty Jean in her home four years. Due to nervous break-down & having to go to hospital, and also finances low, she had to bring her back. Adopted by Mr. and Mrs. Allen Williams Nov. 4, 1935." On the twenty-fifth of July, Rose shared: "Betty Jean Gorney came back this p.m. Had been placed out nearly 4 years." The Williams' family adopted Betty on the twenty-fifth of January 1940. John Potocki said Betty had "very unpleasant memories with this family."

Sixteen-year-old Betty married Stanley Joseph Potocki in 1942. Soon after the wedding, Stanley was drafted. John Potocki shared: "My father and mother were only married for a few weeks, when he was given notice to report for basic training and war in 1942. My parents had just moved into an apartment and were settling in; now their life was turned upside down. It is amazing how life can change in a split second. When Stanley took a train to Camp Phillips and the distant plains of Kansas, my mother soon moved out of the apartment and went back home to live with her parents. Betty went down to live in Mississippi when the division went to train at Camp McCain, Mississippi."

The Germans captured Stanley in January 1945 near Tettingen, Germany. Stanley died in December 1995. Betty Jean Potocki died on the eighth of March 2006 in Cook County, Illinois. She was an avid bingo player.

On the twelfth of October 1932, Mary was placed with Floyd and Vera Fisher of Camden. In October 1933 a state report on Mary Louise noted: "Child is a lovable youngster, bright, doing good work in the 5th grade in the Camden Public School. Attends church and Sunday School. Conduct good."

A state report from December 1934 for Mary Louise showed: "Foster Mother is very fond of this child and is providing a fine home for her." One year later, a state report for Mary Louise shared: "Girl was very appropriately dressed at school, clean and neat. Foster parents stated she is a jewel. They give her chickens or something that she can call her own and just before school started the foster mother let her use her chicken money for a permanent and her hair looked very nice." Mary lived with Floyd and Vera in Fountain County in 1940.

Twenty-year-old Mary married Stanley Metsker in April 1944 at Oxford. Mary died in 1985 in Sacramento, California. Stanley died in 1990 in Indianapolis. Mary and Stanley had one daughter: Pamela Maskel.

Stanley and Betty Jean Potocki
(John Potocki)

CHAPTER 16: RAYMOND LEROY HARSH

On a "nice day" in late May Rose mentioned that Raymond had fractured his arm. Welfare Home records show Raymond was born on the tenth day of October 1918 and was crippled by infantile paralysis, better known as polio. However, Raymond's death certificate showed he was born on the twenty-seventh of August 1917 to a fifteen-year-old, Hazel Harsh, in Rochester. A death certificate identified Raymond's father as an "unnamed white male" who lived at Rochester. Welfare Home records showed that Raymond's father died while he was an infant.

Two-year-old Raymond lived with his eighteen-year-old mother and her parents on Elm Street in Rochester in 1920. Eighteen-year-old Hazel married George Biggs the same year. Hazel died from tuberculosis on the fourth day of December 1924. She was a member of the Church of God.

Raymond entered the Home on the fifth day of June 1926 in "poor" condition. Late in June 1927 Raymond visited his stepfather. Seventeen days later, Raymond was "returned to Home from vacation by stepfather." For Christmas 1927, a nine-year-old Raymond asked for an "aeroplane." An eleven-year-old Raymond lived at the home in 1930. On the sixth of June 1931, Raymond spent two weeks with his stepfather at Rochester. He returned on the twentieth of July.

Judge Robert Miller of Fulton County reported in May 1933: "George Biggs, stepfather of Raymond Biggs, moves the court for authority to have the care and custody of Raymond Biggs for a period of four weeks from this date. Petition granted and the care and custody of said Raymond Biggs is now given to George Biggs for a period of four weeks, or until the further order of court. Said George Biggs is to maintain said Raymond Biggs during four weeks, at his, George Biggs' expense and at the expiration of said four weeks to deliver said child to the Mexico Orphanage at Mexico, Indiana."

James DeWitt shared Raymond's experience with a male caretaker's temper. "He would play ball with us and things like that, but he couldn't control his temper.... We were playing ball. I was the pitcher. And he was batting. And Raymond Biggs, the crippled one, was an umpire at third base. And on the second strike he fouled the ball and Biggs called it a foul, which it was. So then (the caretaker) struck out on the next ball. He started talking to Biggs and walking towards third base, and he still carried the bat. As he was talking to him, he told him: 'No, it was over here.' I was pitcher, so I was in a perfect spot to see it. I saw where it went. And when he told me where it was. I said 'Alright now follow that. If that ball was a line drive and you know it was a line drive where would it have gone if it followed where you went?' He looked, and it would have hit the schoolhouse. But you know what he was doing with Raymond. He took the bat, and he was going like this. I could see it. He stopped. I thought he was going to hit him. Everyone else thought he did hit him. I thought he hit him. But Raymond Biggs was crippled, and he was trying to back up and he fell down. So, everybody swore he hit him. I said 'No.' They said I was brown-nosing. I said, 'No. What I saw is what happened.' But I asked Biggs: 'Did he hit you?' and he said 'No'".

A sixteen-year-old Raymond asked for a "knife or lotto game" for Christmas 1934. In November Rose noted Raymond "has been bedfast a long time." In April 1936, they placed Raymond with Roy Lyle of Fulton County. He agreed to keep Raymond until the tenth of October when Raymond would turn eighteen. But Raymond wasn't there long, and on the twenty-eighth of September 1937, Gail Harsh, the director of Fulton County Department of Public Welfare, placed Raymond elsewhere.

Mr. and Mrs. Lawrence Deardorff, in November 1937, shared with Gail what they knew about Raymond: ".... Stepfather George Biggs remarried and is living in Rochester. Half-sister Dorothy Biggs is living with her father or grandparents. Raymond is crippled by Infantile Paralysis and came to the home June 5th, 1926 in very poor health. He has had such contagious diseases as Measles, Mumps, Smallpox, chickenpox, and whooping cough. Our records show that Raymond's grandparents were very fine people."

Forty-one-year-old Raymond married twenty-two-year-old Ruby Ellen Osborn, a registered nurse, around January 1959. Raymond, a farm laborer, died in March 1959 in Fort Wayne because of health issues related to tuberculosis. Ruby died in December 1999.

CHAPTER 17: PRISCILLA AND BILLY HAWKINS

Rose first mentioned Priscilla on the tenth of January 1935 when she noted that "Priscilla & Annabelle have gone to bed this afternoon-fever & headache." Her first mention of Billy came on the day after the Fourth of July when she wrote that Billy and Priscilla came back to the home after spending the fourth with family or friends.

Priscilla was born on the fourteenth of April 1927 in Peru, the daughter of Arthur Hawkins and Marguerite Louise Kerschner. William "Billy" Arthur Hawkins was born on the eighth of January 1929 in Peru. Twenty-year-old Marguerite Kerschner married Arthur Hawkins in September 1924.

In February 1930, authorities sent twenty-five-year-old Arthur Hawkins and Paul Boldman to the Indiana Reformatory in Madison County for robbing a gas station at Main Street and Burlington Avenue in Logansport. The same year two-year-old Priscilla lived in Miami County with her mother and brother, Billy. They lived with forty-six-year-old Joseph F. Krauskopf and his fifteen-year-old daughter. Marguerite worked as a servant for Joseph. Billy and Priscilla came to the Welfare Home on the eighth day of July 1930 as a result of a court order. Brown-eyed Billy and Priscilla were placed with their grandparents, Mr. and Mrs. William Hawkins, the day before Christmas 1930 at 383 E. Adams Street, Peru.

Officials in February 1931 described Priscilla's health as "Good. Girl's left arm is short, fingers only extending below the elbow of her right arm. Otherwise she is very robust and health. Has been sleeping with her aunt, Rosemary, 17, who was recently married. Now when her Aunt Florence 22 is home over the weekends; girl sleeps with her." The report also noted that on New Year's Day Priscilla's grandmother took her to see her father, Arthur. Her grandparents were described as "Grandfather about 60, not very well but is employed. Is English and very severe in his ideas. The grandmother is also English but a little more lenient."

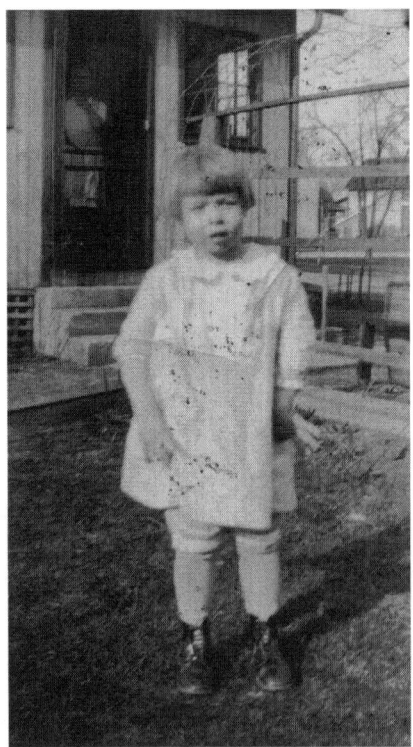

Priscilla Jean Hawkins
1931
(Rose Scholl Family)

In late November 1932 Welfare Home officials recommended that the county authorities visit Priscilla but requested no changes. The grandparents reported that Priscilla's mother "never did take proper care of girl and her brother, William Arthur, four. Grandmother does not visit girl's mother, but mother occasionally comes to grandparent's home." At the time Marguerite "Margery" lived on Eighth Street next to Thomas & Carpenter Grocers and kept house for a Mr. Steward or Stuart.

A May 1933 state report on Billy noted: "Child has lump at outer corner of left eye which sometimes enlarges and seems to cause some trouble. It is said this was caused from being bitten by another child in the Children's Home. Grandparents think child is quite naughty but feel he would be a great deal better if he was not influenced by his sister, Priscilla Jean, who is quite a conduct problem."

A May 1933 state report on Priscilla noted: "Rate of board $2.50 per week. Girl has been treated at Riley Hospital. Health. Girl's left shoulder was injured at birth. Grandmother says girl has a Riley Hospital record…. Child born at Dukes Hospital, Peru." County authorities received recommendations to find a "more satisfactory home for child." The report indicated there were no other family members who could care for Priscilla. "So far as grandparents know there are no relatives of the mother who would wish to have or could make good home for child."

In October 1933, Arthur asked for "leniency" from his ten-year sentence for robbing Joseph Kurger at the grocery store. He was "apprehended in a Kokomo hospital with bullet wounds in his body after he was shot in an attempt to hold up the proprietor of a grocery store at Plum street and Miami avenue."

Their grandparents returned them on the first of June 1934 as they were "unable to care" for them. Authorities described Billy as "quick tempered" and noted that Priscilla's "left arm seems to be paralyzed." In May 1938, they were both placed with their mother at Amboy. In 1934, five-year-old Billy asked for a "little wagon or pair of boots, size 13" for Christmas. The same year, seven-year-old Priscilla asked for a doll or dishes."

On the eleventh of January 1935, Rose noted that Priscilla was sick. By the twenty-sixth of January Priscilla had a temperature of one hundred four degrees, and Rose thought she had the measles. By the first day of February Priscilla was out of bed and feeling better. And the next day Rose noted "Priscilla is fine now."

On a sunny twenty-fourth day of March, Rose commented on the struggles between Dean and Priscilla. "Such a time as the little girls have with Dean. Priscilla says he just disinfeers with all their things. Dean and Priscilla have whooping cough now." Six days later Priscilla, Miss Mae, Alberta, and Rose picked dandelions. Rose noted "Had a good mess for supper." On the twelfth of April, Rose remade a spring coat for Priscilla. On the twenty-second of June, Rose helped Priscilla get her things ready for a vacation.

Marguerite filed for divorce from Arthur in Miami County in September 1935. Her suit claimed Arthur had "been arrested here and taken to Logansport a few days before Christmas 1929 for implications in an automobile theft." Arthur received a ten-year sentence at Pendleton Reformatory. She also said, "he treated her in a cruel and inhuman manner." In November, Arthur asked for and received parole.

Marguerite received a divorce in early June 1937 with Arthur on parole for auto theft. "He was ordered to pay $3 a week support and the two children, who are at the Mexico Welfare Home, are to remain there." A month after the divorce Arthur married Paula Allison. In February 1938, thirty-two-year-old Arthur received a one hundred fifty-dollar fine and a sentence of one hundred eighty days for petty larceny. Arthur died in April 1971 at Tipton. On the eighth of October

1937, Priscilla went to Riley Hospital for an operation on her left arm and shoulder. She left the hospital on the twenty-eighth of November.

Marguerite married Omar Curtis Stewart on Valentine's Day 1938. Two years later, Priscilla and Billy lived with their mother and stepfather in Converse. On the first day of June 1947, Marguerite died in Miami County.

Priscilla married Harold Peter Lehnen. Eighty-two-year-old Priscilla died at Peru on the first day of August 2009.

Bill married Virginia Graham in July 1950. He died on the twenty-seventh of May 2014. They had ten children. Bill founded the Tipton CATV and worked at BRS Mechanical. He loved to fish, hunt, and work in the garden. He was a member of the Kemp United Methodist Church.

CHAPTER 18: PAUL KILE

On a "damp gloomy" Sunday in late January 1935, Rose wrote "Paul Kile came back from a home where he has been for nearly a year." Paul was born on the twenty-fourth of July 1919. In 1920, he lived on Taylor Street in Fort Wayne with his parents, James Kile and Mahala Cressler and a three-year-old sister, Lucille. The Methodist Church welcomed eleven-month-old Paul Kile by baptism in June 1920 at Fort Wayne.

Mahala died in Fort Wayne in 1924. She and James had four children: Lucille, Paul, Norman, and Leonard. Leonard died in March 1919 from tubercular meningitis, and Norman died in July 1921. Five years later, James died of acute indigestion. He worked as a carpenter for the Wabash railroad. James' obituary noted: He "reported for work Friday morning, apparently in good health. About an hour later he collapsed and lived only a short time."

After his death, twelve-year-old, Lucille lived in Rome City with her uncle and aunt, Chester and Eva Nowels. Nine-year-old Paul came to the Welfare Home by order of the court on the twentieth of October 1928. On the twenty-eighth of May 1930, the state placed Paul in the home of an aunt, Mrs. J. Worley, of Peru. She returned him to the Welfare Home on the second of September 1930.

On the tenth of May 1931, the state placed Paul with Viola Workman at Flora. Two weeks later Viola returned Paul to the home because of "stubbornness, would not mind." The state placed Paul with Trest Morton at Amboy on the eleventh of May 1933. A state report showed the boy's conduct was "reported poor. Foster father stated boy was not satisfactory and on 5-25-34 they returned him….. "

Paul Louis "Bear" Kile-1939
(Paula Disbro)

On a rainy mid-June day, Rose made two pairs of shorts for Paul and finished them at nine-thirty in the evening. The day before Thanksgiving Paul left to spend the holiday with "relatives."

Paul's daughter Paula Disbro shared: "I know he wasn't the best child they ever had. He ran away a lot. He talked about getting whipped with a black snake whip because he would run away. He said to go fishing. But he also would go to an aunt's house. He fished until he wasn't able to do so. He got farmed out to different ones but never said much more than that…. He had two brothers, but both died before age 5. My sister remembers him getting whipped and farmed out. Don›t know if whipping was just at orphanage. She says he ran away quite often and usually went to his grandmother's, Julia Ann Elliott Kile. He had a cousin, Betty Maxine Oldham, who was also at the orphanage."

On the eighth of May 1937, the state placed Paul with Walter Curtis at Wabash through the end of 1937. They then placed Paul with William Truitt until the first of June 1939. They later moved the date to September 1939. The same month the Welfare Home wrote a letter to Walter asking that the twenty-five dollars they owed to Paul be sent to them so they could give it to him.

Paul Kile and his sister, Lucille
(Paula Disbro)

Twenty-year-old Paul lived with his uncle and aunt, M.M. and Bessie Warley, in 1940. A fifteen-year-old Betty Oldham also lived in the home. Paul, a high school graduate, worked in a factory as an assembler. He had worked sixteen weeks in 1939 for one hundred fifty dollars.

He married Adella Cecilia Langhammer in November 1945 in St. Louis. From 1950 to 1960 Paul and Cecilia lived at 355 West 7th Street in Peru. In 1950 he gave his occupation as "Molder" and in 1957 and 1960 he listed his occupation as "Fireman."

Paul died on the twenty-fourth of September 1992. His obituary noted "There will be no visitation and no funeral service." Paul served in the United States Marines as an Aviation Machinist Mate First Class during World War II. He was a member of the St. Charles Catholic Church.

CHAPTER 19: FREDDY AND JIMMY LANDGRAVE

On the thirteenth of July 1935 Rose noted that "Jimmy & Freddy Landgrave came." They placed four-year-old Jimmy "in girl's division."

Fredrick Gordon, per his birth certificate, or Frederick per most censuses, marriage, and military documents was born on the fourteenth of August 1928 in Peru to Fred Landgrave and Ada Margaret Jacobs. James Edward was born on the nineteenth of April 1931 at Peru. Their father, Fred, worked as a railroad conductor and was born in January 1885 in St. Paul, Minnesota.

In August 1907, Fred married Maude Vinson in Indiana. They must have divorced, and Fred Landgrave remarried Maude Vinson in St. Joseph, Michigan, in March 1913.

Fred lived on West Seventh Street in Peru in 1920 with Maude. He worked as a railroad brakeman. Also, in the home was a twenty-year-old Mabel Douglas. The same year, a nineteen-year-old Ada Benzing lived in Butler County with her husband David and two children, Marion and Walter. Fred married Geneva Morris at Peru in August 1922.

Forty-two-year-old Fred married twenty-six-year-old Ada Benzing at Peru on the twenty-eighth of October 1927. Three years later, twenty-nine-year-old Ada Landgrave lived on West Seventh

Street in Peru with her husband Fred and one-year old Fredrick. Also, in the home were three Benzing children: Marion, Walter, and William. In October 1932, Ada filed for divorce from Fred and claimed, "cruel and inhuman treatment not only to her but to her two children by a former marriage."

Ada, in September 1934, sued her ex-husband, Fred, for twelve thousand five hundred dollars "in accordance with a purported contract in which Landgrave agreed to pay that amount to her and their two children, James and Frederick." Fred had received twenty-five thousand five hundred dollars related to disabilities because of a train wreck at Richmond in November 1933. Ada married Joseph Louis Seibold prior to August 1938. He was born in August 1907 in Butler County, Ohio, and died in December 1974 at Roann.

Fred managed the Silver Dollar on North Broadway in Peru by October 1934. He advertised "Dancing Every Night. Step To the Latest Music With Dick Downey's Band. Featuring Miss June McCulloch, Vocalist."

In February 1935 at Peru Ada charged Fred with "non-support of two children." Three months later, "Mrs. Landgrave, former wife of the defendant, seeks to collect for services in caring for her former husband after he was injured in a railroad accident. She claims that he failed and refused to keep his agreement to pay her a portion of damages received from the railroad on condition that she return to his home and care for him during his recovery from injuries." The couple had previously divorced.

On the nineteenth of July Rose made a pair of pants for Jimmy and noted "He is the cutest thing. 4 years old." Four days later she wrote: "Freddy & Jimmy's people stopped and gave them some candy." On the twenty-fifth, Rose said Jimmy "is getting along well. Doesn't make any trouble." On the twenty-sixth of August Rose noted: "Jimmy & Freddie went away Sat. came back tonight." On the seventh of September, Rose noted "Since dinner Jimmy & Freddy Landgrave left today."

Fred touted the drug Natex available at Porter's Drug Store in November 1937 and shared how it helped him: "After a bad accident in 1933, in which I sustained several bad fractures, I was left in a pretty bad state. I become badly constipated, suffered so with indigestion, gas, acid-risings and cramps after my meals that I was afraid to eat, was so nervous and had to get up so frequently to relieve my overactive kidneys that I could hardly get any sleep, and was made generally miserable by frequent headaches and dizzy spells.... I'm sleeping like a log and never seem bothered by nervousness or getting up nights. I haven't had a dizzy spell or a headache in weeks and the aches and pains in my back and legs have likewise been relieved. You can depend upon it."

In August 1938, Fred sued Ada and his two young sons. "Sorry that he deeded his residence property to his ex-wife, now the wife of another man, Frederick Landgrave, of Peru, today filed suit in Miami circuit court in an effort to get it back.... Defendant in the action is Landgrave's divorced spouse, now Mrs. Ada Seibold, reported to live somewhere in Ohio. Landgrave says that, on June 23, 1936 'without advice of an attorney,' he had deeded the property to then Mrs. Landgrave and their two children, Frederick Jr., 7, and James E., 10, but that he neglected to attach a provision that he retain a life interest in it. The two children are named parties defendant in the suit, which asks the court to set aside the deed and declare Landgrave sole owner. The plaintiff says that Mrs. Landgrave promised to live in the home and care for their children in spite of the fact that they had been divorced, but that instead she left and married Seibold." In March 1939, Fred filed for a change of venue to move the trial out of Miami County.

Fred's World War II Draft Registration listed Ida Manning of Peru as someone "who would know where he was." Seventy-five-year-old Fred died alone at Peru in January 1962 and was found by a neighbor. Eighty-four-year-old Ada, a widow, died on the fifth of June 1984 at Wabash.

James, a farmer, used the Seibold name prior to August 1952. He married Marjorie E. Ihnen in July 1951. She died in 2001. Seventy-three-year-old James E. Seibold, a widower, died on the twelfth of April 2005 at Fort Wayne. His death certificate listed his parents as Joseph L. Seibold and Ada M. Jacobs. James and Marjorie had five children: Jim Bartoo, Brenda Wadkins, Cathy Harrold, Marian Krom, and Sandy Blakenship.

Some time between May 1944 and November 1947 Fredrick's last name changed from Landgrave to Seibold. He married Donna Belle Siegfred in March 1948. Seventy-six-year old Fredrick Gordon Seibold died in May 2005 at Peru. He worked at General Tire in Wabash and farmed. Fredrick and Donna had two sons.

CHAPTER 20: RUTH AND JIMMY MILBURN

Rose first mentioned Jimmy on the eleventh of February 1935 when she noted that "Jimmy Milburn came back today." On a cloudy day in late April, Rose wrote that "Ruth Milburn was brot back this p.m."

Ruth Vurle Milburn was born on the twenty-fifth of May 1921 in Putnam County, the daughter of William B. Milburn and Myrtle Brunner. James "Jimmy" Clyde Vendel Milburn was born in February 1926 in Tippecanoe County. In 1930, eight-year-old Ruth lived in Monticello with her mother, Myrtle Lansing, brother Jimmy, and a lodger, James Nicholas, a mechanic. They rented the home for twelve dollars a month.

Seven days before Christmas 1930 police arrested James Nicholas "when he engaged in an altercation" with Myrtle and her children. In July 1931, Jimmy was made a ward of the Juvenile Court of White County and entered the Welfare Home. In September, the White County Court found Ruth to be a "dependent and neglected child.... and should be made a ward of the Juvenile Court of White County."

Myrtle died at her son's (Wilbur Maxson) home on the nineteenth of October 1933. Her husband had died two years earlier. Myrtle was married three times to Raymond Lansing, William Milburn, and Joseph Maxson. At the time of her death Jimmy and Ruth lived at the

Welfare Home. In May 1934 they sent Jimmy on a visit with Mr. and Mrs. T.G. Crowder of Peru. Six months later they placed him with Mr. and Mrs. Harmon Hughes in Kokomo. The Hughes returned him on the eleventh of February 1935 due to his being "incorrigible." A state report on the second of May 1934 indicated they had placed Ruth with the Howard Jeffry family in Huntington County. The report noted that she had a seventeen-year-old foster brother, Mark Jeffry, in the home and "some time ago, Ruth's sister, Mrs. Laverne Cline, was in contact with girl. Foster Mother feels this girl is not very good influence for Ruth." The Jeffrey family returned her and noted that she "Would not be subject to discipline and had uncontrollable temper."

Rose mentioned Jimmy a second time on the second of September 1935 when she said: "The kiddies all went to school except Dean and Jimmy." On the second day of July 1935, "Mr. & Mrs. Rarick took Ruth to a home near Huntington for a tryout." On the fifth of September Rose made Ruth an apron. Eleven days later, Ruth was placed with Mr. and Mrs. Robert H. Bucher of Huntington. This placement didn't work out, and on November the fourth, a rainy evening, Ruth was returned because of "incompatibility."

On the twenty-ninth of November Rose reworked a coat for Ruth, and the following day Rose noted "Ruth has been having such a sore throat. I'm going to put her in bed for all day tomorrow." In December 1937, Ruth underwent a tonsillectomy. An April 1938 health report for Ruth and Jimmy showed no active tuberculosis.

On the thirteenth of August Ruth was "taken to Monticello for observation in Boarding School." Thirteen days later, the Boarding school requested Ruth's clothing from the Welfare Home. In September, Geneva Loughry from White County sent a list of Ruth's clothes to the home. Included on the list were: Dark blue twin sweater set, pink blouse, blue & tan skirt, blue & tan jacket & beret, blue & tan blouse, gray tweed skirt, cotton flannel pajamas, golashes, dark green hat, white felt hat, necklace with "R" on it, and two rings. The day before Christmas 1938, Jimmy visited his sister and then went to the home of Carl Witts at Lebanon.

Bessie Campbell, a child welfare worker from Indiana's Department of Public Welfare, wrote in January 1939 ".... so far, James has made a splendid adjustment to this home and both Mr. and Mrs. Witt are very fond of him. We are under the impression that James was given a Wassermann and a pretty thorough T.B. test last year and we are especially interested in this, since James has shown some resistance to the Wassermann test and is quite frightened to think of going through the experience again."

Eighteen-year-old Ruth V.E. Milburn married twenty-one-year-old Curtis H. Miller in September 1939 in Tippecanoe County. Curtis taught French horn in Washington D.C. at the Navy School of Music and later became part of the "Admiral's Band" in California. He was also a State Farm Insurance agent.

Five days after Christmas 1940, Geneva Loughry wrote to the home about Jimmy. "At the present time plans have been made whereby Jimmy will remain in the home of his sister, in Lafayette, under the supervision of the Tippecanoe DPW. It is the plan at the present time to have Jimmy's case studied at the Psychiatric Clinic, which is held in Lafayette.... Will you please give us your knowledge and experience concerning the following items on Jimmy's case and any other items which you feel would be pertinent to this social history: School Record, Personal of Child, Jimmy's problem as you see it."

In 1955 Ruth and Curtis lived in Bloomington where Curtis worked as a "driver." From 1987 to 1993 they lived in Hemet, California. By 1995 they lived in Green Valley, Arizona. Ruth died in December 2002 in Camarillo, California. Curtis died in August 2009 in Ventura County, California. Ruth and Curtis had two daughters: Marilyn and Martha.

Twenty-eight-year-old James Milburn married twenty-two-year-old Betty Schilling on the nineteenth of June 1954. Betty died in July 2016 in Kentucky. City directories showed that James may have lived in Danville, Illinois, Indianapolis, Indiana, and Houston, Texas. A divorced eighty-five-year-old James C. Milburn, a house painter, died on the twenty-third of November 2011 in Beech Grove. His obituary listed six brothers and two sisters who had died before him.

CHAPTER 21: LOIS MILLER

Rose first mentioned Lois on the first of January 1935 when she noted: "Alberta, Pauline and Lois with some of the boys went to Sunday School Class Meeting."

Lois Miller was born to an unwed Walter Elbert Anderson and Florence Adell Miller in Miami County on the first day of September 1919. Walter was born in 1894 and died in 1950. He later married Elva Florence Rinker. Florence Adell was born in 1897. In 1917 or 1918, Walter showed he was a "farm laborer" working in Miami County.

In 1920, a twenty-five-year-old Walter worked in a factory and lived on East Michigan Street in Indianapolis. The same year, twenty-two-year-old Florence Miller lived on Damian Road in Miami County with her parents and two siblings. Also, in the home were two of Florence's nieces, four-year-old Velma M. Howard and one-year-old Mildred M. Howard. It is unknown where Lois was during this time.

Florence married Edward Denton Sherrick at Peru on the twenty-first of August 1926. Edward entered the National Home for Disabled Volunteer Soldiers in Danville, Illinois, for acute bronchitis and other issues in March 1928. He was in and out of the National Home at least twice and left the Illinois home in April 1933.

In April 1930, Florence and her children, ten-year-old Lois and a three-year-old son, Dallas, lived with Florence's mother and sister in Miami County. Thirty-five-year old Florence died of tuberculosis at Peru in March 1933 after being ill for two years. Florence was a member of the Loree Brethren Church. Edward died in December 1942 in Wisconsin.

A June 1933 report showed that Dallas was born the first of February 1927 and came to the home on the seventeenth of June 1933. In mid-September 1933, they transferred Dallas to an institute at Knightstown, Ohio. Dallas returned to the Welfare Home on the eighteenth of July 1938 "after visit with Father.... and Waisners in Howard County."

Officials sent Lois to the Welfare Home in September 1933. Brown-eyed Lois was described as "good natured." On the twenty-first of May 1934, they placed Lois with Mr. and Mrs. Charles E. Waisner at Kokomo. On the eleventh of August 1934, Lois underwent a tonsillectomy. The Waisners returned here in late August 1934 "in order to attend school." They said, "they had no trouble with Lois, and she was returned because of school facilities."

A Welfare Home report in September 1934 showed that officials again placed Lois with the Charles Waisner family near Burnett's Switch in Howard County. By Christmas, fifteen-year-old Lois was back at the Welfare Home and asked for a "diary or autograph book" for Christmas.

On the fourth of January 1935, Rose wrote: "Olivine and Lois are in bed today." On the fourteenth of January Rose said: "Have doctored Lois and put her to bed this p.m." On the twenty-first, Rose wrote "Did not feel well enough to wash. Iris did not go to school this afternoon. Lois went today. Had been out for quite a while." Two days later, Rose noted: "Lois is home with an earache." On the twenty-fourth of January, Rose wrote: "Lois is not in school today. It is so cold and windy." Five days later, Rose lamented "Lois came home from school sick. So now we have 5 patients."

After a busy day of butchering seventeen hogs on the thirtieth of January, Rose wrote "I then washed all the dishes and at 3 o'clock came up and stayed with Lois. Dr. came there & then brought Dr. Malouf 10 p.m. Later ambulance has now taken Lois to hospital,"

The next day, Rose wrote: "I awoke several times thinking of Lois. When I heard Mr. and Mrs. Rarick drive in 1:30 a.m., I inquired how she is – fine so far…. Raricks went in to see Lois. Her side is very sore otherwise she feels real well. She underwent an operation for appendicitis at about 11 p.m."

On the first of February, Rose reported on Lois' progress "The nurses say Lois is getting along very well." Twelve days later, Rose wrote "We are expecting Lois today…. And then Lois didn't come today." The next day on the fourteenth of February, Rose wrote "Lois came about 10:30 feeling fine." The following day after cleaning Rose gave Lois a bath. On the sixteenth, Rose wrote: "After dinner I gave Lois her bath and alcohol rub." Rose repeated the process two days later.

On the twentieth of February, Rose noted that a Mrs. Taggart came to see Lois. After the visit, Rose again bathed Lois. On the twenty-first, Violet and Claudia Fisher came to visit with Lois in the evening. The next day, Rose reported on Lois' condition: "Lois walks around a little but seems all in when she gets up."

On the first of March, the doctor came to check on Lois and Olivine. Rose noted "For the last 2 or 3 days Lois has been up all day." On the seventh of March, Rose finished making a blouse for Lois and noted: "Lois took a walk with Miss Mae." On the fourteenth, Rose started on a new dress for Lois. On the thirtieth, Rose took the girls fishing and noted "Lois caught 5."

On a cool Sunday, the last day of March, Rose assisted Lois with her "Commercial Arithmetic." On the fourth of April, whooping cough was making its way through the children. Rose wrote "Dr. & nurse has been here to see children. Found Lewis positive. Lois also …."

On the eighth of April, Lois stayed home from school with a cold. The next day, Rose shared the following: "We ironed all the boy's shirts, all towels and have a good headway made. Lois and I didn't quit until 9 o'clock." On the twenty-fifth, Lois helped in the kitchen. On the third of May, Rose's children, Robert and Anna Lou, visited her for the day. Rose noted "Anna Lou went downtown and got candy for the girls. Then Lois set her hair."

On the sixth of May, Rose noted "Lois and Thelma go to show this p.m. & boys tonight." Eleven days later, after dinner, Rose and the girls walked to the river. Rose noted ".... Lois & Thelma Gorney got a few mushrooms." On the twenty-ninth of May, Rose cut out dresses for Alberta and Lois. Two days later Rose described the dresses: "Lois has an organdie lavender trimmed in pea green and Alberta is print material." On a warm last day of June, Mr. and Mrs. Waisner visited the home and "took Lois for a ride." On the sixth of September, all the children, except Lois and Dean, attended an evening program at the high school. Rose noted that Lois didn't attend Terrell's class party on the first day of October.

On the second of October, the staff and children, including Lois, Alberta and Bertha, were busy processing grapes and peaches. Rose noted "Cooked grapes. Put pulp thru sieve. Canned 19 qt. juice & 31 qt. pulp before dinner. At 10 mins. to 1 p.m. began making jelly and at 3 had 282 glasses made. Certainly, was kept busy. Miss Mae & I then began peeling peaches. .... Had 32 qt. canned until 7 p.m. Tomorrow will be another busy day."

On the eighth of October, Lois was sick, and Rose wrote "so I mopped kitchen floor and getting dinner. Had toasted cheese sandwiches for everyone-Mashed potatoes, buttered beans and dill pickles for children." Twelve days later, Rose noted "Miss Mae, Lois, June and Marjorie went with Mrs. Hendrix and Bonnie Babcock to the Argos home-coming."

Lois and Myrtle were in bed sick on the thirteenth of November and didn't go with the other girls to see the movie "Freckles." On the eleventh of December, Lois attended a revival meeting with Miss Mae. On the first of May 1936, they again placed her with the Waisners. Lois left the Waisners "to work for wages" on the eighteenth of July 1938.

Lois married Lowell Loop on the fourth of March 1939 in Kokomo. After a weekend honeymoon in Indianapolis, they lived at 1001 North Indiana Avenue in Kokomo. Dallas spent a week's vacation with Lois in late August 1939. Two months later, Lois and Lowell lived at 50 East Jackson in Kokomo. On the third of December 1939, Dallas joined the Mexico Church of the Brethren by baptism. He also spent a week with Lois at Christmas in 1939.

A 1940 city directory showed William and Lois Loop lived at 530 East Jefferson in Kokomo. On the thirtieth of April 1940, Lois took blue-eyed Dallas to live with her. Dallas Elsworth Sherrick died in February 1999 in Wichita Falls, Texas.

Rose and Lois must have stayed in touch as Rose had a picture of five-year-old Joe Loop from 1946. William and Lois's son, Terry, was born in December 1949 at Marion per his birth certificate. However, a birth announcement in a Kokomo paper showed he was born at St. Joseph Hospital in Kokomo. His birth certificate listed his mother as "Lois Smith." Terry drowned in 2000.

A 1953 and 1959 directory showed Lois J. Loop living by herself in Kokomo. In April 1955 one of Lois' friends nominated her for Mother of the Year. The friend said "Candidate for mother of the year: Mrs. Lois Loop. She has given a home to the homeless, guidance to the untrained and love to the unloved…. Hers is a rural home in which much love abounds. She and her family worship at the Galveston Baptist Church."

Lois Jeanette Loop married forty-two-year-old James C. Weaver at Kokomo in September 1964. Forty-six-year-old Lois died in October 1967 in Kokomo where she lived at 518 N. Washington Street.

Her obituary noted that she had two children by an earlier marriage, Terry and Joe, and that she was born on the second of January 1921. But that date doesn't match other birth dates given for her. Her tombstone gives a date of 1919 and Welfare Home records agree with the year but give a date of September first. James Weaver, on her death certificate, listed the names of her parents as "unknown." If he was unaware of her parent's name, it isn't out of the question that he also provided an incorrect birth date

CHAPTER 22: MARJORIE NICE

Rose first mentioned Marjorie in early March 1935 when she made two jumpers for Marjorie out of old dresses. Brown-haired Marjorie Jane Nice was born on the eleventh of July 1921 at Peru, the daughter of Oren Nice and Bernice Marie Quince.

In 1910 an eighteen-year-old Oren lived on West Sixth Street in Peru with his parents and worked as a "fireman" for the railroad. The same year a thirteen-year-old Bernina lived on Colombia Avenue in Peru with her parents. Sixteen-year-old Bernice Marie Quince married Oren at Peru on the twenty-eighth of September 1912. By 1920 Oren Nice, then twenty-eight-years-old, lived in Newberry Township, Miami County, Ohio, in a rented house. He worked as a railroad laborer. Four children and a wife lived in the same home.

Marjorie, the youngest, and four of her siblings -- Woodrow Wilson, Mary Evelyn, Maxine Agatha and Robert Lee -- came to the home on the eighteenth of June 1925. Woodrow Wilson was born in July 1913. By 1940 Woodrow was still single and lived in Berrien County, Michigan. Five years earlier he had lived in Mercedes, Texas. He married Helen Brynn about October 1970 and she died in 1998. Woodrow died in June 2001 in Florida. Mary Evelyn was born in March 1915. In August 1940 she married Ernest Richter. She died in August 2008. Ernest was a car salesperson with Richter Brothers Auto

Sales. Maxine Agatha was born in April 1917 and died in December 2009 in Deschutes County, Oregon. She married Louis Henri Primeau. Louis died in 1994 in California.

Robert was born in April 1919. He spelled his last name as "Nyce." A May 1933 report on Robert, who had a bad left eye showed they placed him with Sam Hower of Grass Creek, six miles southwest of Fulton. The report noted "Robert is a big, healthy, strong boy. He has only one eye and wears glasses." The report also showed Robert was "not in touch with relatives." A June report showed they allowed Robert to go to his father's home in February. By the twenty-first of April 1934, Robert was back at the home. He married Florence Elot in August 1942. He lived most of his life in Kane County, Illinois. Robert died in December 2013. He and Florence had two children: Charles and David.

Marjorie and Frank Korba
(Sharon Brooks)

Sharon Brooks, Marjorie's daughter, shared how Bernice walked out and left the family sometime around 1925. Oren had a good job with the railroad that required travel, and so they sent the two youngest children to the Welfare Home. Marjorie only saw her mother once after that. Sharon revealed that about 1939 Marjorie's mother showed up at the door and said: "I'm your mother." Eighteen-year-old Marjorie said "No, you're not" and shut the door. Marjorie never saw her again. Marjorie's youngest brother, Robert, continued to stay in touch with his mother over the years.

The Nice children spent twenty-three days of May 1929 on "vacation." A court order returned the children to their father in late April 1930. Oren lived at 116 Wabash Street in Peru. On the seventeenth of October 1931 Marjorie came to the Welfare Home from Miami County.

In early July 1933, the Miami Circuit Court ended state guardianship for Woodrow, Mary Evelyn, Maxine Agatha, Robert, and Marjorie. The court returned Marjorie, and perhaps the rest of the siblings to their father, who lived at 356 W. 7th Street in Peru. Marjorie returned to the Welfare Home on the twenty-first of April 1934.

Thirteen-year-old Marjorie asked for an "Uncle Wiggly game or manicure set" for Christmas in 1934. On the twenty-eighth of March 1935, Rose noted "I remade two slips for Marjorie this forenoon." A week later, a cloudy and damp day in April, Rose noted that "Marjorie & Ermaline are sick in bed." Four days later Rose remade a grey coat into a jacket for Marjorie. During a rainy third of July afternoon Rose made a dress for Marjorie. Rose also made a striped dress of Iris' over for Marjorie on the twenty-sixth of July.

Marjorie, Lois, June, and Miss Mae, on the twentieth of October, went to the Argos homecoming. Marjorie's father came to see her on the eighth of December, a Sunday Visiting Day. Only one other parent showed up that day. On the twenty-seventh of May 1936, they placed Marjorie with Dr. and Mrs. Joseph M. Doyle at 567 Fifth Street, Peru.

The Doyles returned Marjorie to the home on the twenty-second of May 1938.

In 1940, an eighteen-year-old Marjorie lived at 122 N. Clay Street in Peru with her father, a coal delivery man, and worked as a housekeeper. She showed she had worked twelve weeks in 1939 and listed an income of twenty-four dollars. Another housekeeper, thirty-one-year-old Fern Brooks, also lived in the home. By 1940, Oren worked as a delivery man and rented a home for eighteen dollars a month. A divorced sixty-one-year-old Oren died in June 1953 in Peru. He had been ill for a year.

Twenty-one-year-old Marjorie married Frank Lewis Korba on the eighteenth of May 1942. Marjorie and Frank soon moved in with his parents. Frank worked at Amtrol as a pipefitter and died in January 1993. A widowed Marjorie died in April 2001 after suffering from Alzheimer's disease for several years. Marjorie and Frank had three children.

Frank, Marjorie and Sharon Korba
(Sharon Brooks)

CHAPTER 23: FORREST NULPH

On the twenty-sixth of July 1935, Rose noted that she and Forrest "mended & patched socks." Forrest Naaman Nulph, born on the twenty-fifth of February 1920, came to the home in September 1926, along with three siblings: Louiszetta, Grace, and Samuel.

His parents were William Nulph and Mamie Siler. At Forrest's birth his father worked for the railroad in "car repair." Forrest was the fifth child born to Mamie. Mamie Siler Nulph married George Heath at Elkhart in October 1925. She was born in 1893. In January 1920 thirty-four-year-old William Homer Nulph and his twenty-six-year-old wife Mamie lived with her parents on Reed Road in Peru. Four children were among the thirteen people in the home: Anna May, Louiszetta, Grace, and Samuel.

Ten years later, a Mamie Pennington lodged on West Superior Street in Fort Wayne with her husband Jack Pennington and a daughter, Fleeta Pennington. William Nulph died in 1958 in North Dakota. Mamie Aerial Hiers died in 1968 in Los Angeles. Her obituary showed nine children: three sons and six daughters. Carol Watts shared how Mamie got divorced and placed the kids in an orphanage until she was remarried.

They placed Louiszetta or Margaret Louise in the home of Wilbur Quinn at Andrews in May 1928. She returned to the Welfare Home in August 1929. Eight months later they placed her with Abner and Ida Alspach at Deedsville. A report on Louiszetta from February 1931 showed her to be in "good" health and "showing good school spirit." By April 1932 Louiszetta lived at Denver with the Harvey Dawald family. Harvey's wife was the daughter of the Alspach family. Louiszetta married Howard Copeland, and in 1940 they lived on Jackson Avenue in Peru with a two-year-old son, Richard. Louiszetta died in July 1972 in Missouri.

Grace Elizabeth went to the home of Howard Tracy at Denver in July 1928. Six days later she returned to the Welfare Home. In April 1930 she lived at the home. Grace married Quincy Hayden in August 1936. In July 1939, she filed for divorce from Quincy. Nine years later a divorced Grace lived with her mother and stepfather on Thirteenth Street in Peru. Also, in the home were her two children Herbert "Buck" Myers and D. Benny. She then married Gordon Smith. Thirty-two-year-old Grace Smith died in March 1949 in rural Miami County. Grace had seven children: Bryce Carter, Mack Allen, Benjamin Hayden, Buck Myers, Carol Watts, Sarah Sue, and Mary Mae.

Samuel Christopher left the Welfare Home in mid-April 1930, probably to live with John Reinholts at Winamac. In February 1932, Samuel returned to the home after the death of John. A month later they placed him with Marshall Smith of Winamac. By 1934 Samuel lived in Los Angeles, California. In October 1940 Samuel enlisted in the army at Indianapolis. He had one year of high school and worked on a farm. By 1955 Samuel lived at Marion and was married to Norma. Ten years later "two bandits, one brandishing a 22-caliber pistol… forced attendant Samuel C. Nulph to hand over $65 and his clothes, shut him in a washroom, and fled." Samuel died in Los Angeles in October 1977.

Ten-year-old Forrest lived at the Welfare Home in 1930. On the twenty-sixth of July 1935, Rose mentioned Forrest when she noted he and Junior Wikel helped make popcorn. At Peru High School, Forrest was a reporter for The Peruvian Yearbook. By 1940 a twenty-year-old Forrest was the Boy's Supervisor at the home. He had completed high school and worked sixty hours the previous week. He showed he had worked twelve weeks in 1939 and had an income of one hundred dollars. Forrest divorced a Patricia in 1945. The same year hazel-eyed Forrest weighed one hundred and sixty pounds with brown hair and a ruddy complexion. He showed his next of kin as his mother, Mamie Hiers.

Forrest, a railroad switchman, married Annabelle in 1946 and they lived at 421 Madison Street in Logansport. He filed for divorce in 1948 citing "cruelty." Forrest married Grace Poyner in 1952 in Wyoming. Three years later Forrest and Grace lived in El Monte, California. By 1959 Forrest was registered to vote as a Republican and lived at 2709 Ontario Street in Los Angeles. Forrest married Helen Nelson in Nevada in 1968. The following year, he sued Helen for divorce in Phoenix. In March 1971 Forrest married Edith Fetner or Edith M. Eden at Imperial, California. He died in June 1998 in Arizona.

CHAPTER 24: JOHN OLINGER

On a snowy third day of January 1935, Rose noted "A new boy John Olinger came this afternoon." John Franklin Olinger Jr. was born on the thirtieth of January 1922 at Peru according to his birth certificate. An Alabama marriage certificate lists his birth year as 1921 and the Social Security Claims index also shows 1921. His tombstone used 1922. A May 1939 wedding announcement and Indiana wedding record showed him at twenty-two years of age, which leads to a birth year of 1917.

He was the son of John F. Olinger, Sr. and Bessie Oldham. In June 1917, John Sr. worked in Peru as a "sawer" and lived at 151 West 1st Street in Peru. He noted that his wife and parents depended upon him. Thirty-year-old John Sr. and a thirty-five-year-old Bessie lived in a rented house on West Second Street in Peru in 1920, with John's divorced brother-in-law, thirty-year-old Clarence Clinton. John worked as "Head Sawer" at a box factory.

Eight-year-old John lived at 204 West Canal Street in Peru in 1930 with his parents and sixty-nine-year-old William Teel, an uncle-in-law of John's. The family rented a home for fifteen dollars a month and didn't own a radio. John Sr. worked as a "sawyer" in a "Wood Working Factory."

In August 1934 John Sr. received a prison sentence from two to fourteen years in the Indiana State Prison North for forgery. In November 1935, officials denied John's clemency request. He received a parole on the twentieth of August 1936. John Sr. died in April 1960. Eighty-one-year-old Bessie died in March 1967 at Logansport.

During a 1988 interview, John indicated that he arrived at the home at the age of ten in 1932 and spent four years there. He said: "Even though some of the boys were ornery, punishment was usually confinement to your room or writing a 1,000-word essay." While at the Welfare Home he "filled the mattress covers with straw, daily for little ones who wet their beds." In July, after a busy day of cleaning, shelling peas, and sewing Rose, noted that "Billy, Priscilla Hawkins, John Olinger, Thelma Gorney and Lewis Roach came back today." The children probably spent the Fourth of July holiday with family or friends.

John had a tonsillectomy in mid-August 1936. On the last day of October, Nina Bauer, the Director of the County Welfare Department, returned John to his parents. Nina Locke Bauer served as the first director for the Miami County Welfare Department.

John married Mary Marlott, a waitress and the daughter of Jesse Marlott and Elizabeth Brown in April 1939 at Peru. Eighteen-year-old John and two other friends had their car hit by a train in June 1939 at the Front Street crossing in Peru. John suffered a bruised arm. The 1940 census showed that he was married and lived at 257 E. 8th Street in Peru with his parents. He worked as a driver and worked 26 weeks in 1939 with an income of four hundred dollars. During the same census, Mary lived with her parents at 608 Washington Street in Logansport.

In January 1941 a married John enlisted in the National Guard Infantry and showed he was a "semiskilled chauffer and driver" of buses, taxis, trucks, and tractors. He was seventy-one inches tall and weighed one hundred fifty-seven pounds. By 1941, Mary appeared in a Logansport City Directory using the Marlott name.

Russell County, Alabama, has a marriage record for a twenty-one-year-old John F. Olinger and sixteen-year-old Barbara Marks, daughter of Archie Marks and Naomi Hubbard for June 1942. At the time John gave his address as Fort Benning, Georgia, and a birthdate of the thirtieth of January 1921. Barbara gave an address of 110 East Canal Street in Peru and a birth date of the eleventh of September 1925. Barbara's mother, Naomi, signed the paperwork to allow her daughter to marry.

John registered for the draft in November 1945. He showed he was unemployed with blue eyes and black hair and weighed one hundred eighty-seven pounds. In May 1957, John discovered the crushed body of a ten-year-old Charles Balsbaugh east of Logansport. Charles died when a tractor overturned on him. John, the engineer on a one hundred and six-car C&C freight train, in July 1969 hit and sliced a car in half near Kewanna. No injuries were reported.

Eighty-five-year-old John died on the last day of January 2007 at Peru. He enjoyed collecting antiques and train memorabilia. He and Barbara had three children.

CHAPTER 25: OLIVINE PARKER

On the fifth of January 1935 Rose noted: "Olivine is sick in bed, so I am taking her share of the work, cleaning, etc." Brown-eyed Elvina Olena "Olivine" Parker was born on the nineteenth day of June 1915 in Carroll County's Deer Creek Township to twenty-two-year-old Alfred Joseph Parker and thirty-year-old Girtha James. A month earlier German submarines sunk the Lusitania, a British passenger ship. Olivine was Girtha's third child. Girtha was the daughter of Albert James and Priscilla McMarlin.

Twenty-three-year-old Girtha James first married Edward Fincher in November 1907. Girtha then married Alfred Parker in August 1913. Girtha and Alfred divorced by early 1918, and twenty-four-year-old Alfred married Mary Josephine Zintz in Indianapolis in May 1918. By 1920, Girtha was married to forty-five-year-old Lewis Gephart. The couple lived in Deer Creek Township with a four-year-old Olivine and Girtha's son, fifteen-year-old Lloyd J. James. By 1920 twenty-seven-year-old Alfred, a construction laborer, lived in a rented house in Indianapolis. In the same house were twenty-six-year-old Mary J. Parker and infant Alice Louise Parker.

Forty-three-year-old Girtha died in late January 1928 from cancer and Bright's disease. The county sent Olivine to the Welfare Home on the twenty-ninth of May 1928. They described her as "Industrious.

Honest, Truthful." A thirty-seven-year-old Alfred Parker, an iron-worker, lived in Baltimore, Maryland, in 1930. He rented a house for forty dollars a month. His forty-one-year-old wife, Tecora Parker, lived with him.

On the ninth of November 1931, the Juvenile Court allowed Olivine, a brunette, to live temporarily with her father. In July 1931, Olivine spent a month with Mr. and Mrs. Russell Green at Rockfield. Two months later, they placed her at Roann with Mr. and Mrs. Hubert Bowman. By mid-November 1931 she was "placed again" with her father Alfred, who lived at 310 North East Street, Indianapolis.

By mid-June 1932 Olivine lived with her father, Alfred. Soon after "Girl left father and went to Anna Murphy.... Indianapolis. Left 1 September 1932, went to maternal Uncle, Charles James, Delphi following...."

A state report from September 1932 showed Olivine: "Needs winter clothing badly. There are only three rooms in the James home. The other one is the kitchen. This is an old frame house in poor repair, poorly furnished and housekeeping poor. Her uncle Chas. James states girl does not seem to care to take his advice and suggestions in matters regarding her discipline. Girl has been able to have a few days' work each week. Goes mornings and returns evenings."

The report even noted that Olivine had a boyfriend. "Mrs. James states she has had a beau or two since she has been with them. One young man whose name she believes is Davis Bloom or Blume, she does not know which, who lives near Flora, has called on girl several times. She thinks this young man seems all right. He has always appeared honorable and has always brought girl back early when he has gone out with her."

The same report noted: "The Uncle feels girl does not spend her money wisely; that she needs clothing badly but is inclined to spend her money on getting her hair put in order and going to shows." Olivine was working for fifty cents a day.

The state agent said: "Visitor also learned from another party that Olivine is paying attention to an old man in the neighborhood about 65 years of age who was reported to Visitor as being "woman crazy…. the reporter stating that this situation is very dangerous for the girl because of man's moral type. It is said the girl often goes near man's home and talks to him. On one occasion she has been seen to go inside his home."

Welfare Home records noted Olivine's heath was "good" in late September 1932. On the first of November 1932, they placed her with her father, Alfred, at Monticello. "Previous reports show that Agent attempted to visit Olivine with Hubert Bowman at Roann, Indiana. The Bowmans told Agent that the girl was allowed to go to her father, Alfred Parker, at Monticello. The father is married again, and she feels that he is able to take care of Olivine. Does not know where the father is living at present but thinks he is in Indianapolis somewhere."

In late July 1934 Olivine was readmitted to the home. And a month later in August, she was summoned to Carroll Circuit Court for a hearing to send her to the Ft. Wayne State School. The same year, nineteen-year-old Olivine asked for a "fleece-lined gloves, size 8 or fleece-lined galosh (medium high heels), size 7 1/2" for Christmas.

On a snowy early January 1935 day Rose noted Olivine appeared on the "sick list." From the fourth day of January through early May, Rose noted that she was sick in bed most of the time. On the fifth of January, Dr. Rendel showed up at supper time to check on some of the sick girls. Three days later Rose wrote: "Since Olivine is sick, I try to get her dormitory work done before breakfast. But this morning Ermaline and I mopped after breakfast."

On the eleventh day of January Rose noted she had a cold and "… took care of the sick girls," including Olivine. The following day

Olivine was the only girl who didn't feel well enough to get up for supper. On the fifteenth Rose noted: "Seems we can't get straightened up from sickness. Olivine is due for a long rest in bed." Two days later Rose noted that with Olivine being sick she had to carry the food to the children's dining room. Ten days later Olivine was too ill to attend church in the evening.

Rose noted on the sixth of February that all the children except Olivine were well enough to eat supper together. Twenty days later, Rose's mother, Elizabeth Blocher, sent a loaf of bread to the Welfare Home for Olivine. On the first day of March 1935, the doctor came to check on Olivine. Fifteen days later all the girls except Lois and Olivine went to the river after dinner.

On the twenty-fifth of March the doctor came and gave Olivine a tuberculous test. Two days later the doctor returned twice to see Olivine and give her a second tuberculosis test. The next day they took Olivine to Peru for an exam.

Rose, on the fifth of April, made Olivine a "bad wolf hat." Five days later Rose went to town in the afternoon and bought candy for her son Robert's birthday and for Olivine. The following day on the eleventh, Mrs. Richey and her daughter came to visit Olivine. Rose noted that Olivine was "growing worse." Two days later on the thirteenth, the girls moved Olivine to the South Room. Dr. Rendel visited Olivine and Rose shared that Olivine "has an abscess on her heel-am poulticing it." On the sixteenth, seventeenth and eighteenth Rose continued "making poultices for Olivine's foot."

In mid-April, Rose made a pair of pajamas for Olivine. Three days later she made her another pair of pajamas and noted the doctor had visited and noted Olivine "had a bad spell." They also had the rest of the children checked for tuberculosis. Rose went to the Fisher family home to get buttermilk for Olivine.

On the twenty-third of April, Rose finished her third pair of pajamas for Olivine. Six days later, Rose checked Olivine's temperature and found it to be ninety-six degrees. They called for Dr. Rendel to come out and check on her. On the first of May, Rose noted Olivine "is getting so weak." The doctor returned to check on her, and Geneva DeWitt came in the evening and spent the night with Olivine. Geneva left the next evening. Geneva had also lived at the home and was two years younger than Olivine.

On a rainy second day of May Rose noted that Olivine was getting weaker and could eat nothing. The following day Rose "took care" of Olivine in the morning, and the doctor came back to see her. The Carroll County Commissioners, at their early May meeting, made plans for Olivine to go to a state institution. On the fifth of May, Rose wrote "Olivine has been quite a care this morning." The next day the doctor came to check on her. Rose wrote: "She is delirious tonight. I did not get to bed until 11. Stayed up until 1:30. I then rang the alarm. Mrs. Rarick stayed over the rest of the night." The next day Rose said Olivine was "very low and she "had to do extra things for Olivine."

On Wednesday the eighth of May Rose wrote: "We took care of Olivine and I have washed for her each day. At 6:25 this eve. Olivine passed away. I called Fetter & Allen. Also called Judge Pruitt of Delphi this p.m. Mrs. Burrows was to her home when Olivine died." The next day Rose reported: "We burned all bedding in sick room and cleaned room well. Talked to undertaker this morning. Blythe of Delphi took the body of Olivine to his Parlors." Olivine's father could not be found. They buried Olivine the following Saturday. Pallbearers included Clifford Baldwin, Charles Fife, Sam Foster, Robert Holsclaw, James Hum, and Rynard Wandri.

CHAPTER 26: SAM, JOHN, AND ANNA QUINN

On the eleventh day of February 1935, Rose noted that Mr. and Mrs. Rarick picked up John and Sam Quinn at Rockfield and brought them to the Welfare Home. A month later Tom Shockley brought Anna Mae Quinn to see her brothers, and Rose noted "I visited with them a while."

Samuel Edward Quinn joined the world on the tenth of May 1926 in Cass County. Miniature golf was invented the same year. John Elmer Quinn joined the family in Carroll County on the fourteenth of May 1929, the same year antibiotics were developed. Their parents were George Elmer Quinn and Grace Popejoy. George, a farmer, was born in 1887. George and Grace married in October 1914 in Carroll County. The boy's older sister, Anna Quinn, was born on the twenty-ninth of May 1923 in Cass County.

In 1930 the Quinn family lived in Rock Creek Township, Carroll County in a six dollar a month rented house. A divorced twenty-seven-year-old Mullendore Quinn also lived in the home. Thirty-three-year-old Grace died at Rossville in late January 1931 from "mitral leakage" of the heart.

On the fourth of March 1935, Mr. Rarick took the Quinn boys to Rockfield on his way to Delphi. On a cloudy eighteenth of November, Rose noted that "Sam had his operation today." In February 1936, Elmer made a few dollars when he hauled a truckload of wood for Robert and Emily Guthrie. Five months later, on the ninth of July, Elmer helped harvest ten loads of clover hay for Charles Harvey. Things must not have gone well, and seven days later "Charles Harvey has granted his farmer, Elmer Quinn, an indefinite vacation without pay beginning Monday. Mr. Quinn will now join the ranks of the unemployed."

In mid-August 1937, Sam, John, and Anna spent part of August with their father. And in December 1938, John and Sam spent Christmas with their father. Ruth Ayres, in June 1939, wrote to the Welfare Home that Mr. and Mrs. Ed Allen were looking for a boy and suggested letting them talk to the Quinn boys. Sam went to their home for a two-week visit and "conducted himself worthily." At the same time, they noted that Anna had been at White's Institute for several weeks.

A month later, Ruth Ayres allowed John and Sam to spend time with their father at his home. On the third of December 1939, brown-eyed Sam, thirteen-years-old, joined the Mexico Church of the Brethren by baptism.

In July 1940 Elmer received permission from Ruth Ayres for Sam and John to spend two weeks with him. Sam also spent a week at the Church of the Brethren's Camp Alexander Mack through a scholarship. A month later John and spent a few days with their father. A welfare report, around the same time, noted that "Sam hauled water during part of the threshing-ring season."

A year later, officials at the home noted: "Sam has helped well with farm team and tractor this summer. His outlook is much better than 2 years ago." Ruth Ayres approved Elmer's request to have Sam and John visit him for two weeks in August.

John left the home on the third of June 1942 and went to live with Ray James of rural Logansport. The next day the Battle of Midway turned the tide of the war in the Pacific. Later the same year a Welfare

Home report noted: "We have heard they are not the best folks for John to be with."

In August 1942, Helen Myer, the Acting Director of the Carroll County Welfare Department wrote: "Sam came in yesterday with his sister and brother-in-law. He said he did not get to Delphi in time to report Saturday. He plans to spend some time with his father but will stay with his sister most of the time. The brother-in-law has a cottage and boats and would like for Sam to stay and look after them, since he works away from home. He said he was anxious for Sam to have a high school education and he would see that he went to school. We believe a plan might be worked out with them, but we will let you know definitely. As least he will be here the two weeks' vacation. John seems quite happy in his new home and we hope it is going to work into a permanent arrangement."

On the twenty-sixth of August 1942, Helen wrote to the home. "This is to advise that we have decided to permit Sam to live with his father this winter. This is his desire, and his father has agreed to make an arrangement for him to live with him and go to school at Rockfield. They will probably be after his clothes Sunday, August 30." A newspaper reported that both Sam and John had returned to live with Elmer.

Sam enlisted in the United States Navy in the March 1944 and received his release in May 1946. He enlisted for the second time in October 1947 and served until July 1956.

John enlisted in the United States Navy on the fourth day of October 1946 and received his discharge on the fifth of August 1949. In April 1948, "John Elmer Quinn, fire man apprentice, USN, and Samuel Edward Quinn, seaman, USN, sons of Elmer Quinn of Rockfield, were among the one thousand officers and enlisted men who were welcomed in Dublin, Eire, today as the United States Navy paid its first visit of courtesy to the shores of the Irish Free State since before World War II. They are serving aboard the light cruiser USS Fresno…."

In December 1948, "Samuel E. Quinn, seaman, USN, son of George Elmer Quinn of Rockfield, Ind. is en route to Beirut, Syria, on a mercy mission to aid approximately 120,000 Arabs who have been drive from their homes by Middle East war. He is one of 360 officers and enlisted men aboard the destroyer tender USS Hamul.…"

A truck driving John died in May 1952 at Fort Benjamin Harrison in Marion County from pulmonary tuberculosis. The same year Christopher Cockerell invented the hovercraft. John had served as a fireman at the U.S. Naval Hospital, St. Albans, New York. His obituary noted he left behind a wife, Dorothy May Marshall, and a son, John Merle, of Indianapolis.

Forty-four-year-old Sam married Lorraine Alice Hopkins in October 1950 at Marion. They divorced twenty years later in Virginia.

When their sister, Minnie, died in December 1970, Sam lived at Flora. In October 1989, a sixty-three-year-old Sam of Logansport received one year in jail for drunk driving. He only served four days in jail and received a ninety-day license suspension. His sister Anna, who lived at 426 Minor Street in Logansport, wrote a letter to the editor of the local paper. "Our Constitution states justice for all. Perhaps someone could explain why one first-time offender for speeding will receive $25 and costs, the next first-time offender will receive $125 and costs. The same is true of first-time D.U.I. offenders–the fines vary from $110 to $260. Why the variance? Also, why is the cash bond receipt made to the offender instead of the individual making the bond? When the offender appears before the judge, all court costs and fines are deducted from the bond money before it is returned. I thought the bond guaranteed the offender's appearance in court–not that his bond and fine would be paid. Any answers?" Sam died at sixty-three at Logansport in November 1989.

In May 1935, Anna's name appeared on a list of Camden 4H club members. Carroll County sent Anna Mae Quinn to the Welfare

Home on the sixteenth of December 1936. Three months later Anna underwent an operation for appendicitis. On the first of September 1937, they placed Anna with Mrs. Alice Wilson of Camden. Later the same month Anna Mae "was taken to an Indianapolis hospital, after falling down the stairs at a local school."

By 1940, a sixteen-year-old Anna Quinn was an inmate in Wabash County at Whites Indiana Manual Labor Institute Home for Problem Children. In June 1943, she was a cadet nurse at Ball Memorial Hospital in Muncie. Anna Mae Quinn of Allen County enlisted in the Women's Army Corp in March 1945. She had four years of high school and was a general office clerk. By September 1946 Anna was married to Frank Blackmond. From 1946-1957 Anna lived with Frank in Erie, Pennsylvania. Anna gave her occupation as "clerk" in 1946.

By December 1961, Anna used the name Anna Mae Griffin. Six months later in June 1962, she went by Ann Mae Ball. In October 1962, Anna used the name Anna Mae Carden. And by July 1964, Anna had married Stanley Walter Komer.

In October 1970, Anna wrote to the local paper regarding "Unemployment Compensation." "I was laid off from National Friction Dec. 19, 1969 for lack of work. My employment compensation was refused at that time because I had quit RBM and had not stayed on the subsequent job 10 weeks. I was laid off over five months without drawing any compensation. Now I am laid off again from National Friction for lack of work. The Unemployment Bureau informs me that I am allowed to file only one claim a year, even though I drew nothing from the first claim. Who pays the unemployment insurance? Also, why isn't the public informed when legislation is passed concerning unemployment?"

Stanley Komer died in February 1982 in Marion County. Anna, a Veteran and widow, died from coronary artery disease in February 1992 at Logansport.

L to R: Candace Smith (Anna's daughter), Anna Quinn, and David Blackmond-
Picture was taken at the funeral of Anna's son, Charles Blackmond
(Selina Uglow)

CHAPTER 27: LEWIS ROACH

Rose first mentioned Lewis on the fourth day of April 1935 when she noted "Found Lewis positive for whooping cough. Three other children were also diagnosed."

Lewis James Roach was born on the first day of March 1927 in Monroe Township, Carroll County. He was the son of Ross Roach and Ruth Elsie Wilson. Ruth and Ross married in September 1924. They had five children.

A daughter, Pauline, was born in June 1925 in Madison Township. Pauline died in February 1979 at Fort Wayne. She never married. Alice Elizabeth was born in September 1928 in Madison Township and died in January 1929 by "strangulation of mucus in throat." A newspaper article noted: "The mother had nursed the child some time previous and had left the baby asleep, but later when she returned, she found life extinct."

Beatrice Elma was born in January 1930 and died in March from pneumonia. Morris Gene was born three days after Christmas in 1931. Morris shared how three families lived in the three-room house and the children were all sent outside during his birth.

By 1930 three-year-old Lewis lived in Ervin Township, Howard County, with his parents and a six-year-old sister, Pauline. By early August 1931, Ross was in jail charged with "criminally assaulting his little daughter, six years of age. The unnatural offence is said to have been repeated several times."

Pauline, Ruth and Lewis Roach

(Morris Herkless)

A local paper reported: "Because of medical opinion during the young farmer's trial that he is bordering on a state of dementia praecox it is thought unlikely that Roach will ever regain his normal mind." Family and neighbors testified about "the young farmer relative to his strange and unbalanced life since he was critically ill with influenza in 1919. From the date of that illness, during which Roach was said by his parents and the attending physician at the time to have been unconscious three weeks, he was shown to have gradually become insane. Mr. and Mrs. Lewis Roach, the defendant's parents, and several of his neighbors testified that he would attire himself in his best clothes and wander aimlessly about the countryside, sometimes staying out all night; that he would visit his father and follow him all day without once speaking; that he would refuse to eat with his parents but would take his meals off to the fields and eat alone; that he would thrust newspaper pictures close in front of other persons' eyes without speaking; that he was uncommunicative to anyone and was morose and displayed no fear or horror over his unnatural acts with his six-year-old daughter; that he frequently would not respond to questions; and that he would tell his father that he paid too much for an article and in the next min-ute, in his father's presence, quote a different price for the same article in discussing it with his mother. Doctors described him as 'a moron and a sexual pervert.' During his trial he sat virtually immobile, staring sullenly and blankly at the table at which he sat."

Lewis, Morris Gene and Pauline Roach
(Morris Herkless)

They found Ross not guilty because of being "insane at the time of the attack and also insane at the time of the trial." After he was in prison for fifteen years, a prison doctor, Dr. P.H. Meeks, "pronounced Roach to be of sound mind." The judge ordered Roach to return to Howard County to face the criminal charges against him. The judge later released Ross. He had to report to a probation officer, H.R. Lookabill, for twelve months and Ross's father promised to help him find a farm job. After being released from prison, Ross married a Lucille and lived in Danville, Illinois. He died in late January 1954 in Danville.

Lewis, Pauline and Morris arrived at the Welfare Home in early 1933. Morris believed all three of them arrived around the same time. On the fifth of December the Carroll County Probation Officer, Mrs. Dora Lyon, wrote to the home regarding Pauline: "The application of Pauline Roach for admission to the Fort Wayne State School having been accepted, I am planning to take her up there sometime next week. Can you bring Pauline to Peru to meet me next Monday, December 11th, so that we may leave on the 11:50 bus, as it is necessary for me to have her in Delphi for a day or two that I may complete her wardrobe and make other plans concerning her entrance into the school? Please bring any clothing that Pauline may have at the school as she will be remaining at Fort Wayne permanently."

In February 1935, they placed Morris with Mr. and Mrs. Carl Herkless at 1600 South M. Street in Elwood. They adopted Morris soon after. On the thirteenth of May, the Raricks took Lewis to Riley Hospital in Indianapolis for a tumor on his upper gum. On the fifth of July Rose noted that Lewis had been at the hospital for seven weeks. By the fourteenth Lewis was back at the home and Rose wrote: "I am helping at first floor and entertaining Lewis in reception room too."

Ten days later Mrs. Deardorff took Lewis back to Indianapolis, and Rose noted they were going back on the twenty-eighth of August. Lewis may have stayed in Indianapolis, since on the fifth of September Rose wrote a letter to Lewis. On the twenty-fifth of September they took Lewis back to Indianapolis, and on the fourth day of November, Rose noted "Lewis went to hospital."

While on the way to the hospital Lewis and Ralph Rarick were in a car accident. Lewis sustained minor cuts and a hand injury. On December the eleventh, Mr. Rarick went to Indianapolis and brought Lewis back from his five-week stay at Riley Hospital.

A March 1939 health report for Lewis noted: "There does not appear to be any active pulmonary tuberculosis at this time. There is, however, evidence of an old primary infection in both lung root areas, which does not appear to be active at this time."

In May 1939, Lewis' father, Ross, wrote to the Welfare Home from his Michigan City prison cell. "I thought I would drop you folks a few lines to see if Pauline and Lewis Roach was still there. If they are would you kindly let me know how they are getting along. I am their father, and I haven't got any word from them for a long time, so I wish to hear from them. The girl will be fourteen years of age June 14th of this year, and the boy was twelve years of age last March 1st. Tell them I am getting along alright. I have been here in the Criminal Insane Colony for seven years and eight months, and I got word how they were only three times. Well I will close hoping to hear from them soon if you please. Yours very truly."

On the first of June Lewis had a tooth filled and "so now O.K. in teeth." On the eleventh of June, Ross responded to a letter from the home. "In answering your most kind and respectful letter which I was glad to hear from you and of my children. The card I received from Lewis was great I thought. You said in your letter that Lewis was entering the Riley Hospital for examination. Did he go there. I sure hope he is alright. I am sure proud of them. I wanted to catch Pauline there to so I wish you would send me the name of the Superintendent and his address so I can write to the State school at Fort Wayne and so I can keep in touch with both of my children. How long has Pauline been at Fort Wayne? Was she to old to be in the home there? Well, it don't matter much for I know they are both in good care anyway. Will you tell Lewis I want him to be happy and tell him I am getting along just fine. I will write him a few lines it is all I can do for him now and thanks to you. Yours very truly."

On the sixteenth of July 1939, Ross sent another letter to the home. "I took the opportunity in answering your's most kind and respectable letter which I received a few days ago. I am glad Lewis is so full of life and getting along fine. I thank you for sending me Pauline's address. I will try to write to her the next time we write. ... This will be all for this time. I will close answer soon. Your's very truly."

On the nineteenth of July, Lewis had a vacation with Mr. and Mrs. Charles Sowers of Wabash "who feel they want a boy for their home." Twenty days later, Lewis was back, and it was noted he was "well recommended, from Sowers who have a man to work for the winter."

In November 1939, Lewis attended a cancer clinic at Riley Hospital. "Doctors looked and had some photos for recording. They seemed pleased that his eyes had not been affected." On the third of December, twelve-year-old Lewis joined the Mexico Church of the Brethren. In November 1940, doctors examined Lewis and said "part of the tumor is visible. It should be watched by them regularly. If we note change, he is to return earlier. In July 1941, they took Lewis back and noted "there had been slight bleeding at times." In March 1942, the Miami Tuberculosis Association noted seven children, including Lewis, tested positive with the Vollmer Patch Test.

By 1940, thirty-nine-year-old Ruth lived at the Carroll County Infirmary. Ruth died in August 1979 in Lafayette after "years of being a semi-invalid."

Lewis married Hertha K. Kraft in July 1948. From 1954 to 1959, Lewis and Hertha lived in Frankfort where Lewis worked in construction. By 1992 Lewis lived at Mexico. Sixty-five-year-old Hertha

K. Roach, a housekeeper at Dukes Memorial Hospital in Peru, died in February 1993 in Peru. She was born in May 1927 in Russelsheim, Germany. Hertha became a naturalized citizen in June 1953.

A widowed seventy-four-year-old Lewis died in November 2001 at Wabash. Lewis' death certificate noted he was a veteran of the Armed Forces and a retired railroad laborer.

CHAPTER 28: EDWARD "JUNIOR WIKEL" SIGLOUSKI

Rose first mentioned him when she said "Junior Wikle got his arm in wringer at old home. Welfare Home and prison records show Edward T. Siglouski was born at Dowagic, Michigan on the fifteenth of April 1923. A Welfare Home report from September 1941 listed known aliases for Edward as Junior Wikley/Wykle and Edward St. Glosky. James DeWitt shared how the children referred to Edward as "Thomas Edward Junior Wikel."

Prison records listed his father as Edward T. and his mother as Hazel. Welfare Home records in 1937 listed his mother as Mrs. Si. Norton of Benton Harbor, Michigan. Edward's death certificate listed both parents as "Unknown."

A Hazel Branch married a Joseph Siglouski in Paw Paw, Michigan in May 1919, and they divorced in Van Buren, Michigan in late October 1923. But divorce records showed Hazel had no children. By 1920, a twenty-two-year-old Joseph Siglowoski or Siglouski, married; was an inmate at the Ionia Michigan Reformatory.

Five-year-old Edward lived with a W.T. and Ethel Wikel at 130 East Canal Street in Peru in early 1930. The census showed Edward as a son of W.T. Twenty-seven-year-old Ethel B. Raines and thirty-four-year-old William Wikel married in March 1915 at Peru. Ethel's obituary showed an Edward Wikel as a stepson. In July 1933, William married Nina McCumber Miller. Sixty-year-old William Thomas Wikel died in 1942 in Michigan from cirrhosis of the liver. There was no mention of a son or stepson in William's obituary.

Edward arrived at the home on the eighth of November 1930. Miami County paid seventy-five cents a day for his care. In 1934, eleven-year-old "Junior Wykle" asked for "roller skates or Popeye walking toy" for Christmas. Late in July 1935, Rose shared that "Forrest and Junior Wikle…. helped to pop corn."

Edward graduated from the eighth grade with a "C" average in 1941. Four months later, Miami County sent Edward to a camp in South Bend. Within five days Edward ran away. By December 1941, Edward worked at the Boston Store in Plymouth. A month later, a minister took Edward to the home on the way to schedule his appendix operation. Peru Township paid for the operation. In June 1942 Edward showed he weighed one hundred sixty pounds and stood five feet seven inches with brown hair and eyes. Edward enlisted in the Navy in July 1942 and received a discharge in April 1943.

In April 1945, Prisoner number 31938 listed an alias as "Junior Wickle." He received a sentence of one to ten years for grand larceny from St. Joseph County. He received a discharge in April 1950. Jasper Helsel of Plymouth received Edward's prison pay. In 1950 Edward lived in South Bend.

Three years later, Edward confessed to Kokomo police a stabbing, fourteen break-ins, and two cases of larceny. Police arrested him in South Bend as he burglarized a Sears store. Edward admitted to stabbing the owner of Mikalas Candy Shop at 207 East Superior Street in Kokomo. He stole sixty-five dollars but didn't remember much else, as he had been drinking.

Thirty-year-old Edward T. Siglouski, Jr., single, arrived at Indiana State Prison North from St. Joseph County on the thirtieth of November 1953. Edward weighed one hundred sixty-one pounds and worked in a restaurant. He listed a Mrs. Nora Helsel of Plymouth as a friend. Prison records showed he had two felonies on his record. Edward had some difficulty adjusting to prison. In July 1954 they sent him to solitary for having contraband. In September he received ninety days in solitary for being "out of place."

A judge "dismissed robbery and the infliction of physical injury on a person during the commission of a robbery charge" in October 1954. In February 1956 they again sent him to solitary for "Insolence." Five months later he received a transfer to the Indiana Reformatory and in November 1957 they released him on parole. In June 1958 he returned to prison as a result of a parole violation. They discharged him five months later. Personal records from the 1953 incarceration noted his mental condition as "fair-epileptic." He didn't smoke or use tobacco or drugs, but he drank.

On the thirtieth of November 1958, Edward received a sentence of two to five years for second-degree burglary. He again listed a friend as Mrs. Nora Helsel of Plymouth. They noted three felonies and three misdemeanors on his record. In February 1960 prison officials disciplined him for having contraband, and in October 1962 he received a reprimand for "horse play". They released him in July 1963, and he provided an address for the South Bend YMCA.

Forty-three-year-old Edward, in May 1966, received his fourth prison term in twenty years for stealing two hundred eighty-nine dollars from South Shore Station. "The judge cited a pre-sentence investigation that showed Siglouski had served a term for grand larceny in 1945, and for burglary in 1953 and again five years later."

In December 1968, forty-six-year-old Edward lived at 223½ Michigan Street, Elkhart, and he received a fine of twenty-five dollars for shoplifting. Sixty-nine-year-old Edward Thomas Siglouski died in March 1993 at Indianapolis. He never married.

CHAPTER 29: ALBERTA SLAGLE

Rose mentioned Alberta on the first day of January 1935, "The roads are very slick. Alberta, Pauline and Lois with some of the boys went to Sunday School Class Meeting,"

Brown-eyed Fatima Alberta Slagle was born on the twenty-ninth of January 1919 to machinist William Thomas Slagle and housewife Vada Marie Britton at Peru. That same year the first radio station -- KDKA AM -- in Pennsylvania received a license. Fatima was the first of her mother's three children to live.

William and Vada Marie married in Custer, Michigan in May 1912. William requested a World War I exception from service based on his "drunken" condition. In 1919, William and Marie lived at 391 W. 7th Street in Peru. One year later, a one-year-old Alberta lived on North Grant Street in Peru with her parents. Some time between Alberta's birth and April of the following year, her parents separated.

Marriage records show that Vada Marie Slagle, not yet divorced from William, married Nathaniel Wilson in Peru on the eleventh of April 1921. William and Vada Marie divorced on the fifth of March 1923 in Mason County, Michigan.

By 1930, an eleven-year-old Alberta lived with her Uncle Harry and Aunt Hazel Downing on Hoover Avenue in Peru. On the twenty-sixth of August 1933, Alberta came to the Welfare Home. She was fourteen years old. The report noted "right name is Slagle. Wilson is name of stepfather."

Rose had a December 1959 picture of Alberta, her husband, and three children. She noted: "The Schwenk family: Alberta (the mother) was about 18 years at the Mexico Home." Rose may have been off with her dates, since Alberta would have only been sixteen years old in 1935.

On the sixteenth of January 1935, Rose noted: "I have just felt terrible all day," but she and Alberta finished the ironing at 10:30 p.m. The following day on the seventeenth Rose made a wool skirt for Alberta after mending eighteen pair of hose and repairing two ironing cords.

On the thirtieth of January, Alberta came down with measles. Rose noted on the first of March that "Bertha and Alberta went home at 3." Two weeks later, Rose noted "I got Alberta's good dress nearly finished." On the sixth of April, Alberta and Bertha attended a "music festival."

While dealing with a sore back on the sixteenth of April, Rose cut out a dress for Alberta. She spent most of the day on the twenty-ninth of May sewing: "Made 4 pair bloomers, a brassiere and mended a corselet. Cut out two dresses for the girls -- Alberta's and Lois'. Two days later on the thirty-first of May, Rose noted "I sewed today and have given advice and helped with the girls dresses." Alberta's dress was "print material."

On the second day of July, Mr. and Mrs. Rarick took Alberta to her aunts for a short vacation. Eight days later, Mr. and Mrs. Rarick brought her back. On a "very warm" day on the thirteenth of August, Alberta started sewing on "her red batiste dress." Alberta finished her dress the next day.

On the last day of August, Rose noted that "Alberta Wilson went home to be with her aunt over Sunday." On the twenty-third of September, Rose "made Alberta a silk longer collar." On the second day of October, they canned grapes and peaches. Rose wrote "Miss Mae & I then began peeling peaches. Alberta & Bertha & Lois helped a little with the 2nd bushel. Had 32 qt. canned until 7 p.m. Tomorrow will be another busy day."

On the eighteenth of October, "Alberta went to visit her Aunt Hazel." On the twenty-seventh of November 1935, Alberta spent Thanksgiving with unnamed relatives. After graduation from high school in April 1937, Alberta lived with her aunt, Hazel Downing. Alberta and Ward Schwenk married on the third of July 1938 at Rolling Prairie.

In 1940 twenty-one-year-old Alberta and twenty-five-year-old Ward lived in La Porte with a one-year-old daughter. Ward worked as a laborer, and they owned an eight-hundred-and-fifty-dollar home.

Ward, a farm hand, enlisted in the United States Army at Fort Benjamin Harrison on the thirteenth of April 1944. Reverend Ward Schwenk, from Three Hills, Alberta, Canada spoke on a Friday night at Argos in mid-August 1951. In Argos, in April 1952 both Reverend Ward Schwenk and his brother, Reverend Glen Schwenk spoke at a church conference at Argos. Their sister, Leona Schwenk, a missionary in South America, had given a speech at the conference the previous year.

At the Undenominational Church at Agros in early October, Reverend Ward Schwenk preached on a Friday night, and his family provided "special music." Reverend Ward Schwenk, from the Prairie Bible Institute preached on the tenth of October at the Argos Bible Conference. "A special feature of the opening service will be music by the Schwenk children."

A newspaper reported that on Sunday at 10:45 Reverend Ward Schwenk of La Porte would give a "Bible Conference Sermon," and at 2:30 Ward would provide a period of Devotion" and the Schwenk family would provide music. Reverend Ward also provided an "evening address" later in the day.

Ward and Alberta Schwenk Family
(Rose Scholl Family)

"In late October 1954, "The missionary offering for the Ward Schwenk family in Africa was $35.00. The Schwenks are well known here from visits to the local meetings." On the seventeenth of January 1955, Ward arrived in New York from Southampton, England, aboard the America.

Ward and Alberta's son, Paul, was born in Bertha, Minnesota in May 1962. Three years later, in October, Reverend Ward, who lived in Clarrisa, Minnesota, was selected to serve as the pastor of the Carmel Baptist Church in Ohio.

Fatima Alberta Schwenk died on the second of April 1995 at La Porte. Her obituary noted she had lived in La Porte since 1977 after she and her husband returned from Africa. They had served in Africa with the Livingston Pioneer Mission and New Tribes Mission.

Ward died on the nineteenth of August 2005 at Michigan City. He also served in the army and received a bronze star during World War II.

CHAPTER 30: ARLENE AND ANITA SPRAGUE

Rose first mentioned Arlene and Anita on the eighteenth of September when she wrote: "Arlene and Anita Sprague came today. 4 and 2 ½ years old."

Arlene Katherine Sprague was born on the twenty-eighth of August 1931 at Geneva and was baptized in March 1932 at Huntington in the Methodist Church. She was the daughter of Virgil Edward Sprague and Edna Lillian White. Anita Mae Sprague joined the family on the third of February 1933 at Plymouth and was baptized in April 1933, also at the Huntington Methodist Church.

Virgil and Edna married sometime after April 1930. They divorced, and Virgil married twenty-seven-year-old Eleanor Harriet Goble in November 1937. Virgil and Eleanor lived at 259 E. High Street in Huntington in 1946, and he worked as a "Service Man." In 1962, Virgil married thirty-six-year-old Frances L. Hartley in Riverside, California.

In 1930 a single twenty-year-old Edna White lived in Geneva, Adams County, with her mother, Labina Chase. Edna married Russell "Ray" Cline in 1935. Ray was born in August 1913 and died in May 1992. Edna and Ray lived at Peru in October 1940. Edna died at Fort Wayne in January 1984.

On the twentieth of September 1935, the Juvenile Court at Huntington said "Finding that the mother of said children has deserted them, that they are being kept by relatives; that the father has made Application to Soldiers & Sailors Orphans Home, at Knightstown, that pending action on said Petition, there is no place where said children can be kept and cared for. That said children are declared to be dependent children and made wards of the Court and ordered placed in the Old Folks and Orphans Home, At Mexico."

Arlene and Anita Sprague
(Christina Carey)

Welfare Home records described both Arlene and Anita as "undernourished." Records showed: "Deserted by mother, who was a worthless character. Father, an ex-soldier and a good man." Five days later Rose noted that she bathed Anita. The same day, staff from a Knightstown institution were at the Welfare Home to see the girls.

Anita's daughter, Christina, did not know of her mother's going to the home. Arlene wrote "I've been trying to remember about orphanage. I do recall after mom divorced dad when my sister & I were a few years old, Mom had hard time taking care of us. I remember her saying she needed to put us in orphanage for short time till she got a job & could take care of us. So, I think that happened."

After sharing Welfare Home and court documents with Arlene, she shared more memories on the situation. "But however, I cannot believe mom was that bad of a person. She was young & worried about our care & put us in orphanage for that reason. She did love us & was a good mother, from the time she got us back for (the) rest of our lives. I can't complain about her love for my sister & I. She was a good mom. But, however, my dad was not the person they said he was. He never gave mom a cent for our care, etc. Nor do I recall him being much of a father. Barely knew him in those days. Why mom divorced him? She said he did not want to work or provide for us. But I can definitely say Anita & I had a very good childhood with mom and my stepfather & I always felt very lucky for that. So, no complaints."

On the twenty-ninth of October, Rose took Arlene and Anita to see the probation officer. Anita and Arlene's parents visited them on the first Sunday in December 1935. Probation officer, Dessie Potts, on the fourteenth of July 1936, had Anita and Arlene "returned to relatives."

In 1940, seven-year-old Anita lived with her mother and step-father, Ray Cline, in Miami County. Ray was a crane mechanic with a one-thousand-dollar income. The Wells County Pilots Association and International Union of Operating Engineers both counted Ray as a member. The same year Eleanor Abbott invented the Candyland game. Seventy-three-year old Edna died on the twenty-seventh of January 1984 at Fort Wayne.

Anita Dunfield died in Kalamazoo, Michigan, on the sixteenth of February 1999. The Social Security Death Index listed the following names and dates for Anita: Sprague, November 1948; Feltz, October 1960; Okeefe, August 1967; Feltz, August 1975; and Dunfield, August

1979. Anita had four children: Theresa Feltz, Christina Carey, Desiree Liszewski, and Anthony Feltz.

Seven-year-old-Arlene underwent an appendicitis operation in March 1939 at Peru. She recovered at her mother's home at 361 North Fremont in Peru. In 1940, eight-year-old Arlene lived with her father and stepmother and stepbrother, Larry, at 833 Wright Street in Huntington. Arlene wrote: "In 1940 I did spend 1 year with my father & stepmother. She had lost a daughter my age, & I guess my being there helped her! I liked her. She was a good person. But I got homesick. So went home soon as I was out of school."

At eighteen, Arlene moved to Chicago and got a job at the Chicago Board of Trade. Arlene wrote "Loved it. Worked in the pit as a page to get messages to stockbrokers to buy or sell. I was 2nd woman hired as only males were allowed. But at the Korean War breakout all the young men left. So, they had to hire women." Arlene enjoyed going to the Dragon Ball Room and dancing to the big bands. She moved back to Indiana in 1953.

Arlene and Anita Sprague-About 1947
(Arlene Siddall)

Arlene's first marriage was to an Arthur J. He died in a car accident a year after their marriage. Arlene then married Arnold Benschnieder and had two children. They were married for seventeen years. Arlene worked in retail while married to Arnold and joined the Theater Guild and spent nine years in the theater. She was five feet ten and typically cast as a showgirl and danced.

She then had a short marriage that she described as "the pitts-big mistake." Arlene married Paul Siddall in Las Vegas in 2006. Arlene and Paul had known each other when she was sixteen. They wanted to get married but felt she was too young. Arlene shared: "So 57 years later we did make it." Paul died of cancer soon after their marriage.

Arlene lives in Fort Wayne and enjoys going to the casino with her daughter and playing cards twice a week.

CHAPTER 31: HAROLD SULLIVAN

Rose only mentioned Harold once when on Thanksgiving Day 1935 after a "fine chicken dinner" she wrote: "Harold Sullivan left for a few days' vacation." Harold Earl was born on the twenty-ninth of May 1922 in Jasper County to thirty-year-old Milton Sullivan, a farmer, and sixteen-year-old Mildred Baker. He was their first child.

Milton Sullivan's first marriage was to Myrtle Mooney in March 1916 in Howard County. A married twenty-five-year-old Milton, in June 1917, showed he had no one "solely dependent" upon him for support. He claimed a military exemption because of "rheumatism" and a "broken shoulder."

In August 1916, authorities arrested Milton and charged him with "assault and battery" on his wife. She accused him of throwing dishes at her. Myrtle went to prison on the fifth of December 1917 for thirty days and received a sixty dollar fine for prostitution. Her mother had gone to prison on similar charges in August 1915.

Milton, in mid-June 1919, filed for divorce from Myrtle after a separation of two years. Twenty-two-year-old Myrtle went back to prison on the seventh of July 1919 for thirty days and received a sixty dollar fine for prostitution.

Milton, in 1919, lived on Wabash Avenue in Logansport and worked as a "laborer." In 1920 a thirteen-year-old Mildred lived on Fitch Street in Logansport with her father, Arthur, and sister, Melvina. In November 1921, Milton filed for divorce from Myrtle and asked for custody of one child. He said she had left their home five days before Christmas in 1918. Some time between November 1921 and Harold's birth in May 1922, Milton married Mildred. They lived at 933 Woodlawn Avenue in Logansport in 1926. Milton and Mildred and possibly Harold lived at 945 Erie Avenue in Logansport, where Milton worked as a "Laborer" in 1930.

By 1940 Milton lived with his brother, William on 14th Street in Logansport. A widowed seventy-six-year-old Milton Leroy Sullivan died in December 1965. A family member said he was beaten to death in his home. But his obituary showed he died in a hospital. His death certificate listed "pulmonary embolis, bleeding into lung and a fractured hip" as the cause of death. The coroner marked the death as an accident, then crossed it out and wrote "natural."

Harold came to the Welfare Home on the seventeenth of December 1934. In late August 1936, Harold had a tonsillectomy. Five months earlier, Adolf Hitler broke the Treaty of Versailles when he sent troops into the Rhineland.

About 1937, when Harold was fifteen years old, a female caretaker at the home physically hit Harold. James DeWitt shared the story on how the caretaker lost her job. ".... One day there was 4 of us just outside of her apartment and 3 of us were separated from the other one and I don't know what he said to her but like I said she was a stout woman.... and she hit him, and he had a boil on his face.... And she hit the boil and it busted.... the blood and the stuff was all over his face, and he started crying. Well she went again, and he tried to duck, and she hit his ear.... When it hit his ear why he really cried, and it really hurt him. These other three guys wanted to go after her. I told them: 'No. No. No. You can't do that'.... I said: 'We'll report it'.... I told them 'Nobody lies. You tell it like it is. If you don't want to go stop now'....

We got over and asked the people where the sheriff's office was.... The sheriff didn't want anything to do with us. He said: 'I can't do anything about it.' He says 'You have to report it there.....I said 'We are here to report it'.... Then he says: 'I can't do anything.' What happened is there was three ladies from WCTU (Women's Christian Temperance Union) talking to a guy that was in jail for drinking. They were trying to teach him a lesson in their way. And they heard us and they came over. The first thing the lady wanted to know was: 'What in the world happened to your face?' I wouldn't let him clean it off. I said 'No, it's got to be just like that.' We told them what happened.... She says: 'We'll take you back.' They had two cars. And I sit with the one that was doing the most talking, and I told her 'They'll just sweep it under the rug.' She said 'No, we'll go in there with you. We are going to tell him we want this investigated and if it isn't investigated then we're going to ask for an investigation.' So, the next morning they had one of the trustees with the superintendent. And I was the last one to be called in. They called each one in separately."

In December 1938, the Welfare Home noted that Harold had been "here in the home except for hiring out until early August 1938. Then was placed by Miami Co. Welfare Dept". Harold returned to the home on the twenty-seventh of June 1939 from the Putnams in Wabash County. After a vacation with William Truitt, Harold left the home to live at the Truitts on the last day of August. A report noted Harold "got along nicely but Truitts were moving," so on the twenty-seventh of October, he arrived back at the home.

In 1939 Harold appeared on the July and August and November and December resident list at the home. He spent the last week of 1939 with Walter Williams of Rochester.

Between December 1939 and April 1940, Harold had seven teeth filled. On the twentieth of January 1940 "Harold went to Williams with the decision of Mrs. Bauer," Miami County Department of Public

Welfare. On the fourth of March 1940, "Harold was back to the home because of mal-adjustment on the part of both he and the Williams." The home took him back to the Williams to get his schoolbooks and clothes the following day. A report from a school official, Mr. Purdue said: "Harold conducted himself as well as you could ask at school." He also appeared on a Welfare Home list for January, March, April, May, July, and August 1940 list.

Five months later, Harold received a discharge from foster care and left to live with his grandfather, Arthur Baker at Peru. During the summer of 1941, Harold lived with A.C. Brenner at Twelve Mile.

Nineteen-year-old Harold died at Peru on the tenth of December 1941. Harold worked at a brass foundry and died from spinal meningitis caused by syphilis. An obituary showed he lived with his grandparents, Mr. and Mrs. Arthur Baker of Bloomfield. Harold was a member of the Mexico Church of the Brethren.

CHAPTER 32: BERTHA VOIGHT

On the sixth of January Rose noted that Bertha was sick and "went to church this morning but not tonight." Brown-haired Bertha Ruth Voight was born on the ninth of February 1918 in Peru. The same year Charles Jung invented fortune cookies. She was the daughter of Fred Voight and Elizabeth Agnes Tubbs. Fred and Agnes married in late January 1915.

On his World War One Draft Registration Fred claimed an exemption based on "Family Support." He worked as a Chauffer for the Crawford Music Company of Peru. In 1920, Bertha lived with her parents and a three-year-old brother Herman on East Eighth Street in Peru. Her father owned an auto repair shop and rented a home.

In July 1927, Fred, a Peru fireman and Agnes had a son Frederick "Charles" Lucerne Voight, and they lived at 152 West 7th Street. Agnes died in January 1929 at Peru from pericarditis with psychosis listed as a secondary cause of death. Fred would die in 1944.

They placed her brother, Freddie, Jr., in the Welfare Home on the eleventh of March 1931. A month later they placed him with Mr. and Mrs. Joseph Conrad at Urbana. He returned to the Welfare Home on the twenty-sixth of April and then returned to the Conrad home on the third of May. The Conrads adopted Freddie in March 1932 in Wabash

County under the name of Chas. Frederick Conrad. He married Mary Blackwell in May 1952 and died in February 2018 at North Manchester.

In April 1930 Bertha was a patient at the Indiana State Sanatorium in Parke County. The institution was better known as the State Tuberculosis Hospital. Bertha came to the Welfare Home on the first of July 1932. On the second of July 1933 she spent time with Mr. and Mrs. Edward C. Irish at 259 W. Main Street, Peru. She was back at the home on the first of September 1933.

Sixteen-year-old Bertha, in 1934, asked for a "bathrobe or house slippers, size 5" for Christmas. After getting sick on the sixth of January 1935, Bertha was still in bed on the eighth. In mid-January, Rose used one of Bertha's dresses and remade it for Louise. On the first of March, Rose noted "Bertha and Alberta went home at 3." Days later Rose converted one of Bertha's jumpers for use by Louise.

Rose, in mid-March, cut out a print dress for Bertha. Bertha and Alberta attended a "music festival on the sixth of April. On the twenty-second of April, Bertha "had teeth filled."   On the twenty-sixth of May, Bertha left for "her vacation." Bertha's aunt wrote to her in early June from Columbus, Ohio. "Dearest Little Bertha: Have been thinking of you lots lately. How are you & how are the rest of the folks. I do hope fine. I heard you were out here in the orphanage so I wonder if you would like to come here & live with me. I can get you a good job & I have a nice place to live. I live alone. I am going to come to Peru soon, so if you would like to come let me know & I'll come & get you. So write me at once and let me no. Lots of love your Aunt Liota. PS.... Will expect to hear from you at once. Please."

On the twenty-eighth of August Rose noted "Bertha Voight came back today." Bertha and two other girls helped Rose and Miss Mae peel peaches on the second day of October. They canned thirty-two quarts. On the first of November, Rose noted "Bertha went to Gishs tonight."

Bertha's aunt wrote to her from Columbus, Ohio, in April 1936: "Dearest Bertha R: Well darling, indeed its a very nice favor to answer your kind letter. Will say I'm so sorry to hear of your sickness had so hoped you would never be troubled with it again. But that's the way the world goes everyone has his or her troubles. I guess you know & understand I've had my share. Honestly Bertha dear, I've answered your letters, so I hope you do get this one. I wondered why you hadn't written to me. This is about my fifth one to you. I wrote you one at Xmas time to Peru. In care of Mrs. Irish. Sure sorry you are going to Rockville. Wish you would go to Ft. Wayne it wouldn't be so far & I'd come to see you often. Please change your mind & go to Ft. Wayne. I know all the Drs & nurses & I do know its much nicer there than at Rockville. I hope you don't go before Easter. Cause I've planned on coming to Indiana then Ivan & I will come see you. I've a surprise for you when I see you. I'm very grateful to Mrs. Irish for being so nice to you dear. But really wished you would have came home with me. Then you would have the clothes & everything you need. You could still go to school. So, if you do go & get out ok. I want you to come to me when you get out well. I am your Aunt & I owe that much to my sister. And Bertha you know & remember, I stood with her and helped her to the end. Glad Herman came to see you honey. Is he a nice boy? Tell him to write me. If everything goes ok, I'll see you Easter Sunday so be a good little girl write more often please. As ever Lovingly Your Aunt Loita …. PS In case any time you should want or need me my telephone No is university 819. Answer real soon please."

They took brown-eyed Bertha to the Indiana State Sanitarium at Rockville in late April 1936 for treatment of her tuberculosis. Two years later, Bertha was a student at Peru High School and involved in "Loyal Rooters, Girl Reserves and the Peruvian." She was also the vice-president of the Commercial Club. In 1939 Bertha lived at 22938 Cherry Hill Road in Dearborn, Michigan. The following year, twenty-two-year-old Bertha lived on Clinton Street in Hammond and worked as a live-in maid for Arthur and Jane Knoerzer and their twin daughters, Jane and Joan. She had an income of three hundred dollars and had worked sixty hours the previous week.

Bertha married Elbert Haworth in April 1941 at the Peru Church of the Brethren. Elbert worked at the International Smelting and Refining Company in East Chicago and Bertha worked at Hirsch Shirt Company. Elbert started basic military training in March 1943 in Missouri. At the time he and Bertha lived at 5643 Sohl Avenue in Hammond. Elbert died in 1960. Bertha died five years later in Lake County.

CHAPTER 33: CLEVO
MAY WILLIAMS

Rose only mentioned Clevo once in her journal. On the eighth of November 1935 she noted: "Mr. and Mrs. Deardorff went after Ada, Lillian & Clevo this p.m." Clevo was born on the sixth of November 1925 to Carl Williams and Ruth Keller in Monticello. C. Francis Jenkins invented the telephoto lens the same year.

In 1930, Clevo lived with her parents and younger brother, Carl, on Lockport Road in Carroll County's Adams Township in a home they rented for seven dollars a month. Blue-eyed Carl was born on the twenty-first of January 1928 near Delphi. Another brother, Clarence, arrived in September 1930 near Burnettsville in White County.

A Welfare Home report from June 1932 showed the children's father incarcerated at Pendleton Reformatory and Ruth, their mother, lived at Idaville. Twenty-nine-year-old Ruth married John Swab in Fall River County, South Dakota in July 1935. A state report from July 1933 on Clevo noted "County authorities consider advisability of girl visiting Grandmother." The report said: "Grandmother states child sleeps with her. Grandmother has some sort of eye infection. Eyes badly swollen and inflamed and discharging a great deal of puss. Visitor explained to grandmother that it is not advisable that child sleep with her, that girl should sleep alone. Grandmother stated she did try to make other plans. The grandparents are hard pressed financially and grandmother is probably not as careful of infection as she should be. She told visitor girl has own towel and wash cloth but visitor doubts this very much."

The same July 1933 report noted Clevo's father, Carl, stayed with his father-in-law, Milton Keller, and helped him dig ditches after his release from prison in March 1933. Carl

Clevo May Williams
(Judy Runk)

said if his ill wife returned from Montana he would be "willing to give his wife another trial for the sake of the children."

In 1940 John lived at Seattle, Washington, with a Ruth Maude Swab listed as "next of kin." He worked for Lincoln Lewis and Clark Company. By 1942 Ruth and John lived in Great Falls, Montana. In 1953, they lived in Astoria, Oregon. Ruth died in 1974 and John died in June 1978 at Broken Bow, Nebraska. Carl Williams died in October 1971 at Monticello.

On the ninth of June 1932, Clevo, Carl, and Clarence were admitted to the Welfare Home. The same year Ole Christiansen invented Lego bricks.

In May 1933 they placed Clevo with her paternal aunt, Clevo Watkins Monticello. The report noted: "Health: Good. Girl has own bed in same room with her cousins, Louise and Jean Watkins, twelve and eleven years of age. At the time of visitor's visit girl was visiting her maternal grandparents, Mr. and Mrs. Milton Keller and her father, Carl Williams, Idaville." The report noted Clevo's mother was "very ill" and in a hospital in or near Great Falls, Montana. They noted her mother "plans to return to Indiana when she is strong enough." Three months later a court order returned Clevo to the Welfare Home.

Judge Ralph McClurg of the 39th Judicial Circuit wrote the home in December 1933 and asked, "Will you please permit Clevo May Williams to spend Xmas vacation with Mrs. Watkins."

On the nineteenth of January 1934, they sent Clevo to Camden to live with the Harvey Crumpacker family. Eleven months later a state report showed Clevo living with the Harvey Crumpacker family one mile south of Camden.

The report shared "Health: Bad tonsils and probably adenoids. Girl shares bed with Lillian Bailey, in same room with Ada Bailey, boarders." The following year on the twenty-second of November 1935 a report noted Clevo had left the Crumpackers …." The White County Court, in November 1935, sent Clevo, Lillian, and Ada Bailey to the Welfare Home from the Crumpackers.

In July, Clevo spent a few days with Mr. and Mrs. Jacob Beaver of Logansport. On the first of September, they sent Clevo to be with Mr. and Mrs. L.B. Lantz of Monticello. In January, Clevo joined eleven other young people in a play, "The Lost Church," at the Guernsey Brethren Church. In November 1944, Clevo served as an usher at the Senior class play "Professor, How Could You?" at Monticello. Clevo graduated high school at Monticello in May 1945. Five months later, Clevo had surgery at Lafayette and lived with Mr. and Mrs. L.B. Lantz in Monticello at the time.

Clevo married Paul Ernest Ruemler in Perth Amboy, New Jersey, at the Lutheran parsonage in September 1946 prior to his overseas departure. However, he never went overseas and finished his military time at Fort Campbell. Clevo lived with Paul's parents during his military service.

In January 1969, Paul and Clevo sold their farming operation located "3 miles west of Monticello." Besides their farm equipment they sold two hundred forty-four head of hogs. A 50th wedding anniversary article noted Paul had retired as a trucker with Hanenkratt Grain and Clevo had retired from the Monticello IGA. In June 1981, Clevo and Paul's son, thirty-one-year-old Ronald Ruemler, died in a motorcycle accident.

Eighty-one-year-old Clevo died at Monticello in October 2007. Her obituary noted: "Clevo had lived in the Monticello, Indiana community for the last fifty-five years. She had also lived in Idaville for six years, Mexico for eight years, Chalmers for seven years, and Otterbein for three years." She was a member of the St. James Lutheran Church in Reynolds. Clevo and Paul had six children: Judy Jones, Barb Bridge, Carol Rowland, Sandy York, Linda Bougher, and Ronald.

Clevo's brother, Carl, was also at the home for at least four months from July through October 1939. In April 1939, "Carl was retained in the 3rd grade." An undated medical examination of Carl described him as "dull," weighing eighty pounds and standing four feet eight inches tall.

A February 1951 letter from Superintendent Henry Swayer to Arthur V. Huffman, Division of the Criminologist at Joliet, Illinois shared: "Carl was admitted to the Home here on June 9, 1932 at which time his father was in the Indiana State Reformatory at Pendleton, Indiana. There is nothing in the records to indicate that Carl was other than a good boy while here at the Home. He was, however, slow in school, had defective speech and poor eyesight."

In May 1939 Geneva Loughry informed the home that physiatrist, Dr. Potter Harshman of Fort Wayne would see Carl again in early June. On the first of June, an x-ray on Carl's teeth showed they were "O.K." On the second of June, Carl was taken to see a psychiatrist, Dr. Potter Harshman. The Welfare Home report noted: "Carl's wearing of his glasses was especially called to our attention as necessary."

In October 1939, Geneva Loughry, from the White County Department of Public Welfare, contacted the Welfare Home and shared they had "made different arrangements for Carl and plan to call for him early afternoon of Tuesday October 31, 1939.… Will you please see that Carl is kept home from school on that afternoon and that his belongings are packed and ready to leave with him?"

Carl married Loveta B. Cox in February 1973. He died in September 2006 in Love County, Oklahoma. Carl worked in maintenance for the Grand Prairie school system and served in the U.S. Army.

On the twenty-third of February 1937, they transferred Clarence to the Fort Wayne State School. In 1940, a nine-year-old Clarence Williams was an inmate at the Fort Wayne State School for the Feebleminded. Eighty-three-year-old Clarence Williams died in March 2014 at South Charleston, West Virginia. His wife, Gladys, passed away prior to 2014.

CHAPTER 34: BOBBY WILSON

On the seventh of August 1935, Rose wrote: "Robert Wilson has come during my vacation." Robert Sherwood Wilson was born on the eleventh of July 1922, the son of Raymond Wilson and Ethel Mae Jamison. A sister, Dorothy, preceded him in May 1921, and Bettie June followed in January 1925.

On the twenty-ninth of January 1918, twenty-one-year-old Raymond went to Canada and signed up for military service. He gave his present address as Ingalls and said he was born the day before Christmas 1896 in Quebec, Canada. Raymond, a cook, listed a brother, Leslie Wilson, as his next-of-kin in Holly, Michigan. Raymond had dark hair, grey eyes and a fair complexion, with a flag and shield tattoo on his left shoulder and a dagger and woman tattoo on his right forearm.

Raymond married Ethel in late October 1919 in Cass County. Four months earlier World War I had ended with the signing of the Treaty of Versailles. By 1920, Raymond, a blacksmith's helper, and Ethel lived in Logansport in a rented home on Market Street.

In August 1924, Ethel filed for divorce from Raymond. She claimed Raymond had "failed to provide for her and their two children to such an extent that she has been forced to seek aid from her grandmother, stepfather, the township trustee, and charitable institutions.

Her husband is physically able to provide for this family." "Cruel and inhumane treatment" was also alleged.

On the fourteenth of April 1925 Raymond arrived in Ontario. They sent Bobby to live with his grandfather Wilson in Holly, Michigan on the twenty-fifth of June 1927. On the twenty-fourth of October Bobby was returned to the Welfare Home by Emma Barry, the Miami County Probation officer. For Christmas, a four-year-old Bobby asked for an "automobile."

Emma Barry placed Bobby on the seventh of February 1928. On the second of March, Bobby returned to the home. Later the same month, Emma placed Bobby again. On the twenty-first of April, Emma returned Bobby to the home. On the twenty-sixth of August 1929 the Miami County court sent Bobby back to his mother.

Bobby also spent time at the Indiana Boys' School. He entered on the seventh of January 1926 and lived there through the twenty-seventh of June. He also spent time there in October 1927 and February 1928 through August 1929.

Thirty-six-year-old Raymond Sherwood Wilson died on the third of September 1933 in Seattle, Washington. Ethel Marie Berger, forty-six years of age, died in late February 1951 at Peru. She had married Charles Frederick Berger prior to 1940.

Thirteen-year-old Bobby returned to the home on the fourth of August 1935. A report noted "Is somewhat hard of hearing as the result of measles when young. Also has had mumps." The report said: "Ran away several times, the last one being Oct 20 after which time he was apprehended in Michigan and returned to Miami Co. jail and sentenced Nov 12 to Plainfield." The report showed Bobby spent most of the summer hitchhiking between the homes of relatives.

Bobby must not have liked the home much, and seven days later Rose noted that "Robert Wilson ran away last night and have heard nothing of him." Bobby ended up in Anderson and on the seventeenth of August Rose reported: "Mr. Rarick & Mr. Dubois went to Anderson but did not bring Bobby Wilson back. He had escaped them just a few minutes." On the twenty-first Rose wrote: "Had a phone call that Bobby Wilson is being held at Anderson. Roland will go for him in the morning." Roland returned the next day with Bobby. Bobby's uncle, Ross Wilson, lived in Anderson. Two months later on the twentieth of October, Bobby ran away again.

Robert Sherwood Wilson
(Debra Johns)

Robert graduated from Peru High School in 1940 and then joined the U.S. Army Foreign Service, where his service received a "Top Secret" classification. He received an Honorable Discharge after being injured. After his discharge he spent twenty-plus years working on oil drilling rigs in Texas. He then spent three years as a drilling contractor in North Africa. After five years working for Delco Electronics in Indiana, he spent twenty-plus years working in Alaska, much of the time working at Kulis Air National Guard Base as a security officer. Robert married Rebecca Brenton in April 1966 at Kokomo. She died in 1999. He married a second time.

Robert died on the thirtieth of January 2016 at Lafayette. His obituary noted that "Robert had one brother who died at birth. He had two sisters and never had the chance to have a life with them because they were born during the depression. His parents separated and his mother was unable to support any of the children. They were all adopted out to different people. They were very small at the time and never knew one another. He never saw his sisters again until he returned from the service in 1943 and they never became very close because of living apart so long. He lived most of his life in adopted homes and orphanages in Mexico, Indiana. A few years later his mother remarried, and he was invited to come live with his mother on a farm."

Debra Johns shared the following about Bobby: "Bob was a WWII veteran. He was in Special Forces. He was very intelligent and very strong willed. He had a keen mind till he passed. He traveled the world and lived in Alaska. He was a very proud Veteran and loved his country whom he served with all his heart. He was very outspoken and didn't mind telling you his thoughts. He often wrote to politicians, including President Obama and gave his two cents! He had a very hard time living in the 21st century. He was of the old school. Bob collected stamps. He put together model airplanes, cars and even did woodworking. He loved to make clocks. His hands were gnarled with arthritis, but that didn't stop him. He loved mechanical toys, especially ones that did funny things like press the hand and 'let air.' He supported an orphanage, 'Boys Town.' Bob loved life. He loved his mother; he had a picture of her hung up in his office. Bob wanted his electric wheelchair donated to another veteran when he passed. He was a loving and caring man. I was there the last day he was alive, and he said he 'didn't want to die.' He was strong willed and fought to live to the end."

EPILOGUE

When I visited the former site of the Welfare Home in the summer of 2019 all that remained was a marker, a sunken depression in James McConahay's yard, and a small concrete block shed.

M.E. Miller shared "…. It is true there have been many discouraging times in the past…. but it behooves us as Christian citizens to look back over the years and see the vast amount of good that has been delivered from our efforts. Such as fine substantial Christian characters that have been developed in some of the boys and girls who have gone out from the Home, some of them being ministers of the gospel, evangelistic singers, businessmen, farmers, and many founders of good Christian homes.

Years later at a reunion for the children and staff; a former superintendent commented he was surprised at the lack of attendees. James DeWitt didn't think it was surprising at all. Reflecting on home life some eighty plus years later, when asked what he learned from his experiences James shared: I learned a lot. So many of them learned the wrong direction. I fought it. A lot of them didn't. That was the difference. A lot of them got in trouble coming out of there. We were considered the home boys. In town it wasn't a respectful name for it. We never caused troubles. I don't know. But none of us could help it. If you don't have any parents. You don't have any. You feel it all the time. Even at church. We would go to church and they had amen pews they call them.... Boys sit on one side and girls on the other side. They treated us as like we were lepers almost.... But at the church you could never sit anywhere but there. Everything was wrong about it....They never had boy scouts or girl scouts there. Most of the time I was there they had ministers as superintendents. Not one of them, to the boys anyway, ever talked about church or anything. I thought that's what they wanted them for."

Reunion at Spencer Park, Logansport 1975
Rose Scholl, Avanell Swartzell and Alfa Crumpacker.
Avanell was born in 1916, has no name on her birth certificate.
She came to the Orphanage in May 1925.
(Rose Scholl Family)

Geneva DeWitt, her husband Slim Messer and Orville Bailey
1991 Reunion
(James DeWitt Family)

Marker at the former site of the Welfare Home

BIBLIOGRAPHY

1910 United States Census. Retrieved from: www. ancestry.com.

1920 United States Census. Retrieved from: www. ancestry.com.

1930 United States Census. Retrieved from: www. ancestry.com.

1940 United States Census. Retrieved from: www. ancestry.com.

Anderson, Karen. 2019. Email communication.

Argos Reflector, The. Retrieved from: www.newspapers.com.

Binnie, L., Sherman, O. & L., Gottman, C.L. 1989. A Century of Service 1889-1989.

Brown County Democrat. Retrieved from: www.newspapers.com

Carroll County Comet. Retrieved from www.newspaperarchive.com.

Chronicle Tribune. Unknown. John E. Terria Personal Collection.

Church of the Brethern [sic] Mexico Indiana, 150 Years.

City Directory. Retrieved from: www.ancestry.com.

Constitution and By-laws of the Old Folks and Orphans Home, Mexico, Indiana.

Daily News Democrat. Retrieved from www.newspaperarchive.com.

Death Certificate. Retrieved from: www.ancestry.com.

Delphi Citizen. Retrieved from www.newspaperarchive.com.

Delphi Journal. Retrieved from: www.newspaperarchive.com.

Denton, Marjorie. 2019. Personal correspondence.

DeWitt, James. 2019 Interview.

Disbro, Paula. 2018. Email communication.

Edinburg Daily Courier, The. 1945, July 9. Retrieved from: www.newspapers.com.

Find A Grave. https://www.findagrave.com.

Fort Wayne Journal-Gazette, The. Retrieved from www.newspapers.com.

Fort Wayne Sentinel, The. Retrieved from: www.newspapers.com

Gospel Messenger, The. 1928, July 28. Retrieved from: https://archive.org.

Haughton, Lisa. 2019. Interview.

Hepworth, Glenna. 2019. Email.

Hepworth, Glenna. 2010. Retrieved from: https://www.ancestry.com.

Hoosier Democrat, The. Retrieved from: www.newspaperarchive.com

Huntington Herald, The. Retrieved from: www.newspapers.com.

Huntington Weekly Herald. Retrieved from: www.newspapers.com.

Indianapolis New, The. Retrieved from: www.newspapers.com.

Indiana State Archives. State Prison Files.

Indiana State Archives. Deaf School Files.

Johns, Debra. 2019. Personal correspondence.

Journal & Courier. Retrieved from: www.newspapers.com.

Kokomo Tribune, The. Retrieved from: www.newspapers.com.

Leedy, Janet. Ringmaster.

Logansport Press, The. Retrieved from: www.newspapers.com.

Logansport Morning Press, The. Retrieved from: www.newspapers.com.

Logansport Reporter. Retrieved from: www.newspapers.com.

Los Angeles Times, The. Retrieved from: www.newspapers.com.

Miller Bechtold Families. 2013, February 8. Mexico Orphan's Home. Retrieved from: http://millerbechtold.blogspot.com/2013/02/mexico-orphans-home.html.

Montana Standard, The. Retrieved from www.newspapers.com.

Patrick, Kathy. Newspaper clipping.

Patrick, Kathy. 2019. Email.

Peru Tribune Obituaries: 2015. Retrieved from: http://incass-inmiami.org/miami/vitals/deaths/peru_tribune_obits_2015.pdf

Pharos Tribune. Retrieved from: www.newspapers.com.

Pharos Tribune. 2016, December 7. Front seat to history: Pearl Harbor survivor remembers attack 75 years later. Retrieved from: http://www.pharostribune.com.Potocki, John. 2019. Phone Call.

Potocki, John. One Last Mission. Retrieved from: http://onelastmission. com/brothers.htm.

Scholl, Rose. 1935. Personal Journal.

Siddall, Arlene. 2019. Personal Correspondence.

South Bend Tribune, The. Retrieved from www.newspapers.com.

St. Louis Star and Times, The. Retrieved from www.newspapers.com.

Swayer, C. Henry. Memoirs of Mexico Old Folks and Orphans Home Church of the Brethren

Timbercrest Home Senior Living Community Archives. North Manchester.

Timbercrest Newspaper. Unknown. Mexico Orphanage: Was good place to be in Depression Years; Wabash Resident Reports.

Wikipedia.com. The Little Colonel. Retrieved from: https:// en.wikipedia.org/wiki/The_Little_Colonel_(1935_film).

World War I Draft Registration. Retrieved from: www. ancestry.com.

World War II Draft Registration. Retrieved from: www.ancestry.com.

Yearbook. Retrieved from www. ancestry.com.

INDEX

Gary Scholl (Rose's grandson), James DeWitt and Eric Flora
2019